W9-BND-651

Saint Peter's University Library
Withdrawn

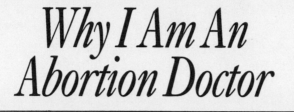

Why I Am An Abortion Doctor

Suzanne T. Poppema, M.D.
with Mike Henderson

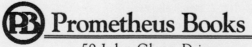

Prometheus Books

59 John Glenn Drive
Amherst, NewYork 14228-2197

To Peter, Andrew, Will, and Jenna,
four of the most wanted children ever.

Published 1996 by Prometheus Books

Why I Am an Abortion Doctor. Copyright © 1996 by Suzanne T. Poppema and Mike Henderson. All rights reserved. No part of this publication may be reproduced, stored in a retrieval system, or transmitted in any form or by any means, electronic, mechanical, photocopying, recording, or otherwise, without prior written permission of the publisher, except in the case of brief quotations embodied in critical articles and reviews. Inquiries should be addressed to Prometheus Books, 59 John Glenn Drive, Amherst, New York 14228–2197, 716–691–0133. FAX: 716–691–0137.

00 99 98 97 96   5 4 3 2

Library of Congress Cataloging-in-Publication Data

Poppema, Suzanne T.
    Why I am an abortion doctor / Suzanne T. Poppema and Mike Henderson.
       p.   cm.
    Includes index.
    ISBN 1–57392–045–2 (cloth : alk. paper)
    1. Abortion services. 2. Abortion. I. Henderson, Mike. II. Title.
RG734.P65   1996
618.8'8—dc20
                                                   96–2445
                                                     CIP

Printed in the United States of America on acid-free paper

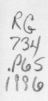
RG
734
.P65
1986

Contents

Introduction

It comes up now and then in casual conversation. I travel frequently. My husband and I are wine-lovers and we go to a lot of tastings. We're mixing socially and inevitably the question is posed:

"What do you do, Suzanne?"

"I'm an abortion doctor," I respond. "I run Aurora Medical Services, north of Seattle. I started it about ten years ago."

Perhaps I elaborate by saying that we help women with choices they make about their own bodies. We counsel women, yes. We explain to them all the options involved with their pregnancy. A former patient, for example, came in during the spring of 1994 for abortion counseling only to discover for the first time that she was carrying a full-term fetus.

"But mainly," I tell them, "we terminate pregnancies—hundreds of them. And lately we've been one of about a dozen clinics throughout the country testing the drug Mifepristone; you know, the French abortion pill, RU 486."

Mifepristone may, for several reasons, prove to be the undoing of the antichoice movement in America. On the other hand, the United States has shown an ongoing, bewildering resistance to accepting—much less embracing—information having to do with birth control, sexually transmitted diseases, and sex in general. Relatively few Americans, for example, know of the existence of a very simple "morning-after" birth-control pill. That's why I tell people about the method (discussed in chapter 17) every chance I get. I tell people whatever they want to know, and I let them know up-front. There's no need to couch the subjects of sex, birth control, and abortion in euphemisms, tactful explanations, or qualifying terms. It doesn't bother me at all that some find my work appalling. They waste their time trying to engage me in debate since my view on women's right to choose concerning matters affecting their own bodies is intractable.

I'm an assertive person, and always have been: assertive as a toddler who knew what her mother wanted; assertive at age three, nearly scaring the life out of relatives; assertive all through Catholic schooling in rural New Hampshire, waiting tables in a small-town cafe, staring down the challenge of Harvard Medical School, fighting the war machine, discovering my feminist core, and realizing my professional dreams.

I was up front and assertive the day I explained to my young sons why I would be wearing bulletproof gear to work in the mornings. But then my sons, my husband, and I know all about each other. We're all open about ourselves, and I can't imagine living any other way.

I'm sure there are many who simply can't imagine how anyone could ever become an abortion doctor. The antichoice folks who oppose women's reproductive rights often cast such physicians as diabolical at the very least and suitable hard targets in the extreme. Assaults on abortion doctors and clinics, as I'll discuss, have gone on undenounced even by well-known representatives of such institutions as the Catholic church. I've known some of the doctors who have been gunned down by such antichoice zealots as the shotgun-armed ex-minister who murdered Dr. John Bayard Britton in Pensacola, Florida, during the summer of 1994. While such violence has forced some abortion clinics to close, those of us who can afford the security measures and the increased insurance payments have redoubled our efforts to perform our vital public and health-care service. As a board member of the National Abortion Federation, I can vouch for the commitment of my peers to the cause of women's sovereignty over their own bodies.

But beyond that I only can tell about the making of this particular abortion doctor. So, why did I choose this profession? What was in the background of this woman who became an abortion doctor, and what brought her to embrace the beliefs she now holds inviolable?

I'll also tell you exactly what I do—and don't do. I'm first and foremost a doctor, and much of my career has been as a practitioner of well-integrated family medicine. I've delivered hundreds of babies and I've treated women, men, and children for virtually every common affliction.

But there are some things I simply won't do. I don't, for example, appear on screen during TV interviews such as the ones I did after it was revealed in 1994 that my clinic would be an abortion pill test site. Showing my face would make me more vulnerable to some extremist finding dubious biblical justification for gunning me down in the supermarket checkout line. I also don't countenance misinformation about women's reproductive rights and the realities of abortion. That's why I was extremely pleased when producers of the TV program "Law and Order" called to ask me for technical advice about a 1995 episode in which an abortion doctor is slain.

The script-writers had erred on a few critical points, which scarcely surprised me. So much of what people—even the well-meaning ones—believe to be true about abortion issues comes from biases and false assumptions. The true test, it seems to me, of whether grandstanding patriarchal politicians such as Bob Dole,

Phil Gramm, and Jessie Helms truly want to say they're what they call "prolife," but what in fact is "antichoice," is to turn the argument around. Would any of these men want to put the matter of their own reproductive organs in the hands of a women's political caucus? Do these antiregulatory, anti-big-government types honestly believe that the state should decide about what the individual does with her—or his—body? Or are they really just playing to the cheap political seats when they wave the "prolife" banner? Are they really just trying to placate a patriarchal right-wing faction, the agenda of which seems to have more to do with subjugating women than with outlawing abortions?

I'll address some of these themes and other issues that affect women as they attempt to assert the essential demand of feminism: that they be treated as equal human beings. I'll also discuss how I came to form the beliefs and values that are reflected in my work today. Then I'll describe precisely what happens and doesn't happen in the abortion clinic. Those who have been influenced over the years by the antichoice attempt to frame the abortion controversy in terms of "baby-killing" may be surprised to find the truth about what goes on inside a supportive, well-run clinic. I'll also report about the promise brought by the testing and pending approval of RU 486 for its use in the United States.

This book, including the comments in the appendices, is very frank, assertive, and honest. I'll talk about my own abortion experience and a miscarriage that preceded the births of two of the most wanted children in the world. This is in stark contrast to the millions of unwanted children born each year, unappreciated and consigned to lives of abuse, abandonment, and hopelessness, if not torture and starvation.

It would sound noble to assert that the fundamental reason for what I do is the alleviation of suffering among unwanted children. But that's only part of why my work means so much to me. The main reason is that I believe women shouldn't have to explain to governments, religious groups, those of another opinion, or the patriarchy at large that they've made a decision to deal with a condition of their own bodies. They certainly shouldn't have to explain anything to the doctors who are sworn to care for them. Women who choose to end unwanted pregnancies deserve to be cared for with the same regard for their needs and their dignity as anybody else who seeks medical care. They needn't have to answer to the value judgments of others. Their decisions about their own bodies should be honored.

That's precisely what I do. I honor and care for patients who want to end pregnancies. I'm an abortion doctor, and I refuse to mask my work in qualifications or apologies. What I do is right and good and important. Perhaps my story will appall some, but it also may inspire others, particularly the young women who need to know that the struggle between feminism and the patriarchy has not been in vain.

Part One

Waiting

1

Wednesday, 9 A.M.

Dawn turns a page of *Time* magazine and rearranges herself in her chair. Across the waiting room a nervous auburn-haired woman laughs quietly, as an acquaintance makes a nearly inaudible remark. Dawn, twentyish with spraying yellow curls and mall clothes, has been an early arrival. She's already done the requisite paper work and will be among the first patients to be treated this morning. She'll be looking for a ride home when it's over because her boyfriend has had to hurry to work after dropping her off.

The conversation between the other two women, borderline silly, has something to do with corn flakes. But the subtext, of course, is abortion. From their demeanor, it's impossible to tell which of the two is here to end a pregnancy and which is the loyal friend and designated driver. Across the room another woman seems to squeeze the warmth from a latte cup while an older woman who later proves to be her mother passes her a cellular phone. An eavesdropper surmises that the call is to the younger woman's day care because the questions are about a baby.

Two more women, younger still, appear at the thick glass security window that has greeted our patients in the aftermath of the murderous attacks on East Coast abortion clinics soon after Christmas 1994. The women announce themselves to a staff member but fumble with the electronic catch on the door to the waiting room. The dozen chairs in the waiting area have filled by 9 A.M. of a typical Wednesday, and already they're emptying as women who are beckoned for counseling yield their seats to new arrivals. Among the latter are another young woman and her male partner, who take five color-coded forms from the reception desk and forge ahead with paper work. He reads while she writes.

Two of the forms ask standard medical clinic information. A third is an authorization sheet (see Appendix A) and the fourth explains the abortion procedure. The fifth sheet, the blue one (see Appendix B), is what distinguishes my clinic from the general family practice I helped operate during most of the 1980s. The blue sheet takes a measure of the woman's emotional wellbeing prior to the abortion: "How are you feeling about your decision?" "How are you feeling about safety?" "What are your thoughts about how you will feel during the abortion?" "What are your thoughts about how you will feel after the abortion?" "How much support do you have from others in relation to your decision?" Each question allows for three different responses. By skimming these surveys we can determine immediately whether the woman is emotionally ready before we check her physical condition.

The key word on the blue sheet is "you." At our clinic we're concerned first and foremost about the individual, the patient, the woman. Her decision is the only one that matters to us. The blue sheet and subsequent interviewing may suggest that a client hasn't quite come to terms with her decision. On occasion I have counseled such women to go home and think further about the decision they are making. I must admit that the need for such reflection is extremely rare because virtually all the women who come to us have made their decision. For whatever reason—or for no reason they wish to articulate—they come to end unwanted pregnancies. Their right to exercise that choice is a fundamental freedom that we do not question. But it poses such a threat to the power of the patriarchy that the right to choose to end unwanted pregnancies has faced repeated challenges. It is testament to the strength of Dawn and hundreds of thousands of women like her that they will put up with just about any threat from antichoice zealots in order to exercise the right of sovereignty over matters affecting their own bodies.

The lights from the ceiling illuminate the deep red field of a Middle Eastern prayer rug at the center of the waiting area. On the surrounding walls are muted art works with feminist themes. In abrupt contrast is a wall-hanging near the doorway. It reads: Family Planning Services Available. The services are listed in nonalphabetical order and one could conclude that this randomness in some way is meant to deemphasize service number seven, which is abortion. In fact, "abortion" is buried in a list that includes "free pregnancy testing," "annual exams," "pap spears," and "vasectomies" for a simpler, less sinister reason. The term "abortion" is positioned where it is because that was the only way the painter could fit all the service wording onto a sign of its size.

Yet, despite the thirteen services we offer at Aurora, the practical matter is that abortion is what we mainly do. Shortly past 9 A.M., Dawn and what now are about eight other women are waiting to see our staff members. Within a few hours there will be nearly a dozen fewer unwanted pregnancies in the world. The occasional nervous laughter aside, there is resignation in the eyes of these women, even the ones who try to break the brief monotony of the occasion with light chatter and small talk with loved ones. No one revels in ending an unwanted pregnancy. To believe that they do would be to imagine that women would willfully become pregnant for no other reason than to be able to come in for an abortion. The antichoice crowd and the patriarchy that gives it encouragement would love to have everyone believe that this is true. At the same time, even those who grudgingly support highly restricted abortion rights seem to feel that pregnant women should have to "pay" in some moralistic way for their predicament. Advancements such as the drug-induced abortions the clinic is helping to test have led some to suggest that it could somehow become far too easy for women to end an unwanted pregnancy. With an abortion pill, how could the woman possibly suffer in a manner commensurate with the bad thing she's done? Despite what we know about sex (and Americans know shockingly little), there's an inference drawn by some that the pregnancy came about unilaterally: "She got pregnant" is the verdict. Or, more preposterous still: "She got herself pregnant."

But we who believe in choice know this to be true: Dawn and the other women we will see on this Wednesday aren't different from any of the thousands of other women who have come into the clinic before them. They are pregnant, period. They have come to us in order to deal with a condition of their sovereign bodies. They are pregnant and they don't want to be. Their pregnancy isn't an issue for the state to mitigate. It isn't a matter for their church to judge. It isn't even something to which their husbands or partners can be privy if the woman doesn't want it that way. The choice to end the unwanted pregnancy isn't negotiable. It belongs only to Dawn and the other women. Realizing this no doubt accounts for the resignation in their faces and the strength with which they invariably greet the procedure.

Dawn is particularly strong, especially when considering the trauma she suffered during two prior procedures.* The most recent, Dawn tells us, was in New Orleans, where the attending physician actually yelled at her during the procedure. She says it got so bad that she started to black out and tried to climb off of the operating table. It never ceases to amaze me that, despite such bad experiences, women still will summon the strength to end subsequent unwanted pregnancies. But I and my colleagues hear repeated stories about abortion

---

*It is important to note here that women who have multiple abortions are not "using abortion as birth control," but, in fact, are having an unfortunate number of contraceptive failures.

procedures performed indifferently or with something bordering on malice. Every time we hear such a thing we resolve to redouble our efforts to honor these women for what they've chosen to do.

Several of those who arrive as Dawn is called for counseling will spend the better part of two hours at the clinic. Some will thumb through magazines. A couple passes the time by sliding a tape of *Driving Miss Daisy* into the VCR. In one very interesting sense this Wednesday is not at all typical, namely, the ethnic variety of our clients. An African-American couple sits near a Native-American woman, with an Asian-American couple across the room. Since our location is in North Seattle, most of our patients are white.

When summoned to a counseling room, it is presumed that Dawn has already read the the white sheet: "Abortion is a very simple and safe procedure. It takes an average of 10 to 15 minutes to perform. First the physician will do a bimanual exam (using one hand on the abdomen and two fingers in the vagina) to determine the size and position of the uterus. She then inserts a speculum into the vagina so that the cervix comes into view. Up to this point the procedure is identical to your annual exam . . ."

A lot of times the counseling session proves to be a good time for us to listen. This counseling session is for informed-consent education and obtaining information, and it is a time to review the woman's options if she feels this is necessary. Some women want to explain to us their reason for being in the clinic. Maybe they want to justify what happened or apologize for their behavior. It's heartbreaking to realize that certain factions of society have equated unplanned pregnancy with something akin to a sin that must be confessed. The single act of listening can mean so much to a client. Our bulletin board is restocked on a monthly basis with letters from former patients who have written to tell us how glad they were that "you listened to me," "you weren't judgmental," "you answered all my questions," and "you put me at ease." During the counseling sessions we never ask women to explain the circumstances of the pregnancy, why they think they became pregnant, or with whom it occurred. We just let them know that we support their decision and will help them in any way we can.

It's been about seven weeks since Dawn's most recent menstrual period; her pregnancy is not very far along. After her counseling session she's taken to one of our operating areas: a simple, ten-foot-square room where she reclines and places her feet in stirrups. The hard, cold steel is softened and warmed by lamb's wool padding. The lighting is muted except for the illumination I'll need for the procedure. Music is an option. To the extent it doesn't affect my ability to perform the procedure, ritual involving friends and symbols can even be part of the abortion. Some women set up small altar-like areas of cloth and crystals, other women play special music, many burn candles.

My spoken approach seldom varies, not after having performed some twenty thousand abortions. Normally I pose some small talk, perhaps inquiring about the patient's given name. I ask Dawn if she has brought someone to drive her home afterward and she explains about her boyfriend and her job. She hopes she can scare up a friend to come and get her. I decide not to pursue the matter. She's in relatively high spirits under the circumstances and wants to know whether it will be all right to go to work the next day. I usually advise patients that they may feel all right but that they may also not care to be around people right away. "See how you feel," I tell her, and we commence the procedure.

I tell her that I'm going to insert the speculum and after doing so I ask her if it's tolerable. She says it is. A staff member who assists me then cleanses her cervix with a mild iodine solution. "I'm going to use a little cloth," I tell her, "to wash the germs away from your cervix." This takes but a few seconds, at which time I tell her: "I'm going to be giving you an anesthetic now to make your cervix numb. You may get some come-and-go cramping as I do this. But you'll find that the cramps only last about three or four seconds each." Dawn is doing very well. Her eyes close now and then. She seems to be meditating for a few moments, alternately using breathing exercises.

"The anesthetic I'm using," I advise her, "will sometimes make your ears ring and your heart start to pound a little bit. So if that happens it's not anything dangerous at all. It's a normal response to this kind of medicine, and the sensation will pass within a couple of minutes." Dawn indicates that such physical sensations "are nothing new to me," and it's anyone's guess what she means by this.

"Next," I tell her, "I'm going to be stretching your cervix just a little bit, so you'll feel some pressure and some mild cramping. But it shouldn't be anything that hurts a lot. So if it does, then please tell me because I can fix that easily." She still seems relaxed. Seconds later I tell her that the stretching of the cervix is accomplished and "we're more than half way done now." Dawn reports that she feels all right and is continuing to concentrate on her breathing. I get no indication from her physical responses that she's having any pain at all.

"Now you'll hear a loud noise from a machine," I warn her as I activate the suction device. "I'm inserting a plastic suction tube now and you'll feel a little pulling and tugging as I empty your uterus." The noise, similar to that of a small electrical generator, prevails for several minutes. "Everything's going just fine," I assure her, warning her about a dental-procedure-like sucking noise that will be caused by a piece of tissue briefly blocking the suction tube. When the piece clears the tissue continues to flow through the translucent suction tube and into a large glass container. I can tell now that the procedure is typical of abortions of this term of pregnancy.

"Now there will be a little more of the tugging and pulling," I tell her, but Dawn doesn't seem to notice it much. "Now your uterus is beginning to empty much more rapidly," I report, "and you may feel more cramping. But that's a very good sign. It means you're not going to bleed very much and it means we're almost finished. I'm going to stop just briefly and give your uterus a rest, so you'll hear that really obnoxious sucking noise. I'm going to let you rest for about thirty seconds. Then I'm going to do one more check to see to it I'm not leaving behind any lining tissue inside that might cause you problems later on. This will take about one more minute and then we'll be done. But you've pretty much felt as bad as you're going to feel."

SAINT PETER'S COLLEGE LIBRARY
JERSEY CITY, NEW JERSEY 07306

A minute later I assure her that her uterus is clamping down just as it should be. Seconds later I pull the suction tube away and announce: "We're all done." Dawn's eyes are closed but her brows bend and her mouth corners curl upward to indicate relief. The condition that had preoccupied her for several weeks has passed. She has gone back to what she wanted to be. Given her age, the time no doubt will come when she'll want to be pregnant. For now she's not pregnant anymore.

"Any cramps you may have should be gone in about five minutes," I advise her. "I'm going to step out now and check that I have all the tissue, and I'll be right back." In a nearby lab I strain the tissue from a glass container where it has collected during the procedure. To the untrained eye the tissue possibly resembles the residue that would approximate the color, texture, and volume of a single pureed strawberry. But after so many procedures I'm quickly able to find the sac and even discern embryonic detail and the minuscule start of an umbilical cord. Women are asked on the preconsent forms whether they wish to see the tissue. They may respond "yes," "no," or "maybe." Dawn is among the majority who simply will rest a few minutes, get back into street clothes, go to the waiting area, and depart without a backward glance. If they cry—and many do— it's usually after the procedure, when a staff member and I are talking with them and telling them how well the abortion has gone. The full range of emotions can prompt the tears. As we'll discuss in later chapters, women invariably are seized by guilt and shame when they come to see us. That yields to anxiety and, on occasion, fear. Then comes the relief that follows the procedure.

With some women there's also resolve: Never again will I allow myself to be in this position. Such a view has been echoed through the centuries, as women have struggled in every culture and at all times to abort pregnancies they knew they couldn't keep. Dawn is but another heroic woman in an endless connected procession. Patriarchies past and present have endeavored to keep women from managing the matters of their own bodies, the great irony being that it remains a supreme advantage to society when women abort unwanted pregnancies and thus reduce the misery that swells with the numbers of unwanted children.

At the end of the so-called abortion controversy what we're left with is the misery. For me, running an abortion clinic and teaching others to do this work is the best I can do to help alleviate misery at every level of society. I came to this realization early in my career. My husband and I traveled to some of the least developed regions on the globe during the late seventies. I witnessed firsthand the persistence with which little girls are undervalued compared with boys, and how women are subjugated. To try to assimilate what enslaved women must feel, I donned a chador. So doing, I learned what it feels like to be enveloped in black cloth the way millions of Muslim women are restricted: rendered indistinguishable and all but invisible in ancient cultures where sexual inequality is considered among the holiest of traditions.

I witnessed the near futility of imposing birth-control standards in parts of the world where women fear they'll never bring healthy children to an age of probable survival. I've seen women and children in every stage of malnutrition, starving alongside the adult males who "maintain" the societies. My odyssey of politicization led me to Denver, where I worked in city clinics serving Mexican and Asian Americans. This experience showed me firsthand the forces that shape the limited options of the poor. I relished the role of family doctor because it seemed to me to be a singular position from which to address many of the pressing needs of society: I could keep the pregnant mothers healthy and counsel them about how to give birth to and rear strong children. The healthy kids would do better in school—would excel and help break the cycle of poverty. Within a generation or two my work would have brought great social consequence.

But during my ten years of family doctoring, what I saw instead were the ugly social encroachments that attend poverty: child abuse by alcoholic parents, exploitation of kids for sexual purposes, emotional abuse, and abandonment. In Denver and Seattle I witnessed the steady weakening of the social infrastructure by right-wing political administrations and their patriarchal admirers. I feared for what might prove to be the futility of my work. That the family-doctor years took an emotional toll is evident if only in the fact that I seemed to undergo a nearly daily reassessment of my career priorities: One day I would resolve to dedicate my remaining years to working with the kids of substance-abusing parents; the next day it would be victims of incest; and the next I'd be out to mitigate domestic violence.

What was the common theme? Gradually it occurred to me: In virtually every society where a wanted child is greeted by a healthy, accommodating family, that child can expect incredible life advantages—physically, emotionally, socially, and economically—compared with an unwanted child. My goal, then, became that of helping the women—the Dawns of the world—who, for whatever reason, would choose not to continue a pregnancy. If I could abort unwanted births, then I could help prevent unwanted children and help mitigate the human misery that attends them. Being a full-time abortion doctor would work not only toward achieving greater social goals; it also would reassert, from my standpoint, the right of the individual to make decisions that affect the sovereign human body. This is a fundamental human right, and one utterly lost on most, if not all, of those who advocate antichoice. Men who never would imagine consenting to government control of their sexual organs or their health in general are perfectly willing to legislate that control over women. This is done under the guise of "protecting unborn children" and with the convenient disregard for the health, education and other human needs of the unwanted who are born. We hear in every national political campaign "protect the unborn," "rights of the unborn," "baby-killers," and the like. Now, with few exceptions, the Republican party has been taken over by the antichoice bloc. The real possibility exists that a man could be elected president and bring to his office a burden of political debt to that faction of society intent on driving abortions underground.

It's a sobering thought to ponder. On the other hand, the better prospect is that the promise of drug-induced abortions will help put an end to the harassment of women and health-care providers. That way no Dawns of the future will have to be burdened by the shame and guilt imposed by the antichoice factions of society. Perhaps we're more than a few years away from reaching such an ideal. But I have reason to be heartened that the cause of women's reproductive rights is moving ahead with irresistible momentum. I also know full well from my life odyssey that the prochoice cause and the general condition for many American women is far better now than it was just a few decades ago, when I became a very wanted child of parents who seemed to love one another from the moment they met.

2

An Independent Child

Much of what we do and become as adults never occurs to us clearly as children. The fact that I became a doctor—specifically an abortion doctor—is scarcely the result of any fanciful thought (much less deep thinking) as a child. Indeed, the mere notion of abortion was foreign to me during my formative years. It simply wasn't in the ken of a kid from rural New Hampshire, of Dutch and French-Canadian ancestry, and educated with the rigidity of a twelve-year Catholic school curriculum.

Largely by the power of my own will, my formative years were an inalterable march toward the knowledge and independence that later led me to pursue the work that I find so worthwhile. From my earliest recollections I knew and understood that if I worked hard and was dedicated I would succeed at what I chose to pursue. It simply never occurred to me—not until the early seventies, and indeed not until I met a man who was providing abortion counseling and care a continent away—that I would choose to help ease the burden of the world's pressing social and political problems by helping

27

women assert their sovereign right to end unwanted pregnancies. It would prove to be a calling fraught with personal and professional difficulties, but the rewards have far outweighed the obstacles. The greatest reward has been the ability to proceed in my work with the full support and understanding of a loving family. And it was family that presented one of the great strengths of my formative years.

The very earliest recollections I have are from when my family still lived in Holland, Michigan, near the western edge of the state. This was my home until age three. My dad's father (with parents and two brothers) had come over from Gronigen in the northern part of the Netherlands. Names such as Poppema that contain a double-consonant followed by "ema" are common there.

My father's side of the family arrived in the United States prior to the turn of the century, leaving the Holland of the Old World for the utterly American Holland, Michigan, of the new. The latter was an enclave of Dutch immigrants, with most of the people who shared my father's early years being Dutch by heritage, Dutch Reform by religious preference, and nearly uniformly blond and blue-eyed. Vestiges of Old Country values couldn't help but have revealed themselves, but the emphasis among these new arrivals was *assimilate, assimilate, assimilate*: act American; be American. So my dad never learned Dutch. I think it was pretty common at the turn of the century for many new arrivals to forsake the native language. The children of such individuals never spoke or heard the native language at home. Their parents had willingly taken on a new country as their home. All wanted to fit in as quickly as possible.

My dad met my mother in her native Quebec City toward the end of World War II. He was stationed in Quebec at the time and would soon to be on the way to Burma with the signal corps (the precursor of the OSS and CIA). He agreed to go out on a blind date with my mom, who didn't really relish the notion of dating an American: it was her opinion that Americans were much too full of themselves. To her mind Americans projected an attitude that insisted everything was—or had to be—"bigger, better." In fact, she went out with my father merely as a favor to a friend. Apparently it was a fortuitous evening for both of them. After just one date they decided they were the right people for each other. Two years later they were married, but of course a lot happened in the meantime.

Dad spent most of the war in India, in Delhi and Calcutta, and Mom waited for him in Quebec. Her side of my family, French-Canadian, can trace itself back to arriving in the New World in the late 1700s. Prior to their migration, some of the family members were well positioned socially and politically, employed as accountants for the king. It was never made clear whether they came over to get away from the Revolution. The family name, in any case, was Pomerleau.

The social structure of Quebec during my mother's childhood fell into two distinct groups: one either was a French-speaking Catholic or an English-speaking Protestant, the latter historically having all the upper-class white-collar jobs. The Catholics were the more common workers, and hence felt oppressed by the English-Protestant hierarchy. Then there were those Catholics who were held under such control by the local priests that they felt oppression from both sides. This control took several forms. Children of certain families were designated to be "given" to a church vocation as a priest or nun. The attempt was made to see to it that Catholics married Catholics. Or, if they were to marry outside the church, a contract was called for, the pact intended to see to it that the non-Catholic would agree to rear children as Catholics.

The factions typically remained separate, with little mixing even on holidays. So the Pomerleaus represented something of an exception, what with my mom, from a family with seven children, growing up next door to an equally large English-Canadian family. For this reason they wound up speaking one another's languages and knowing each other's customs, which helped my mother block out a lot of prejudicial thinking about English-speaking Protestants. It seems that proximity can have a lot to do with acceptance.

My mother, in any case, was the granddaughter of a prominent family physician whose home was in a village outside of Quebec City. In fact, she was the grandfather's favorite, partly because she was often a sickly child obviously in need of considerable medical attention. She was favored to the extent that she actually lived with her grandparents for a while and would go on medical rounds with her grandfather. One of my maternal uncles is a surgeon. Moreover, my own father had always wanted to be a physician, so that may account somewhat for my interest in becoming a doctor.

The wealth of my mother's family was considerable for the early decades of the twentieth century. Her grandfather, for example, bought a house for his daughter as a wedding present, and provided the servants. My grandfather was involved in accounting and banking. That left him vulnerable at the dawn of the Great Depression, when the family quickly lost nearly all its assets. I can remember quite vividly my mother talking about having gone from living amid the luxury of keeping maids in the house to having so little money that they couldn't heat the house. She would speak now and then of winter conditions so bitter that snow would actually blow into the house through cracks around the windows. The fall from wealth and status, not unlike what many suffered during the Depression, must have had a lasting effect on Mother.

My mother's childhood somewhat foreshadowed my own experience. The thing to do if you were a Catholic daughter of good family background was to be sent to the Ursuline nuns, a boarding school where you were so restricted that you were allowed to get out physically and see your parents only once a month. At other times your parents would have to visit with you through the Ursulines' grille, as though you were in a jail or at confessional. That's where my mother lived for months at a time. It was where the curriculum extended beyond learning a bit of French history and writing to include such apparent requisites as the art of embroidery and the ability to order servants in the proper manner. Such was the extent of instruction, most of it having little if any practical, much less professional, use. Matters were quite different for the boys. The custom was to reserve the advantages of higher education for them, the understanding being that none of the girls would go beyond high school. My mother did, however, receive some practical training from taking secretarial courses for a couple of years. Then she took a job in an office, though she hasn't worked for pay since she married my dad.

My parents, then, who are Donald and Rachel, met in 1944 and were married two years later. I was born in 1948. At about that time my dad was working nights and going to school in East Lansing at Michigan State, studying what ultimately became known as forestry engineering. My mother was, in effect, left with being something of a single parent for much of the time. Moreover, she was living in a non-French-speaking, blond-haired, blue-eyed Protestant enclave while only too obviously being a brown-haired, brown-eyed, French-speaking Catholic. The contrasts were acute enough so that social life wasn't easy for her. That, by the way, has much to do with how I came to speak French before English: Left isolated from much of the community, she spoke to me in French all day.

The master's degree my dad earned was related to forest management, which is what led our family to New England and the only home I lived in after that—the only house my parents have occupied since the day we arrived there in 1951. For lack of a town nearby (Pittsfield and Rochester, where I went to school, are some fifteen miles away in either direction), "rural New Hampshire" was about the most accurate way to describe my home. Even with the encroachment of suburbia through much of New England during that era, our area remained as rural and picturesque as the foliage photos in travel brochures.

The move happened after my dad got a job offer from a man in Boston whose business, the New England Forestry Foundation, owned a lot of land in New Hampshire. Somehow the job included the house, which could be occupied by the family rent-free. My mother initially hated the situation, certain that she could never abide living in such a remote, wooded environment. She'd always been accustomed to the civility of cities, and her early commitment to life in rural New Hampshire went just this far: "All right, we'll live here for six months and then we have to move." In time she embraced the place, realizing that she wouldn't be able to live in the city again under any circumstances. Knowing of her initial objections, I find it amusing but gratifying to note that, after nearly half a century, they still occupy the house, exquisitely interdependent in their mid-seventies.

An advantage of leaving Michigan and being in New Hampshire was that all my mother's relatives now were back within driving distance. Quebec City was reachable in a few hours. That, of course, meant the relatives could visit us, as they did on the occasion of one of my earliest recollections. It was when I made myself "disappear" one day after we'd been living in New Hampshire for six months. We occupied about sixty acres, and after such a brief occupancy my parents still didn't really know the whole lay of the land. I was hiding behind an old stove in the barn, playing hide-and-seek—or I thought I was playing, in any case. A large party of my Quebec relatives was visiting. One of them was exceedingly nearsighted, and seemed to be looking right at me. My childish thought was: "Isn't that nice that he's playing this game with me? And he can see me." So I stayed there for hours, refusing to give up the game even though all around me hysteria reigned. The family called the fire department and the relatives proceeded to thrash about trying to find me. After nearly three hours I decided to come out. Of course it caused a huge uproar. I got smacked by my mother. Both parents were sobbing and my grandmother was crying and yelling at my mother for hitting me.

The fact that I remember the incident so well makes me feel that the experience must have been terribly rewarding for me. I got to cause such a stir and be the center of attention. I suppose it made me appreciate just how much power a child could wield, though in fact it isn't even my earliest memory. I actually recall certain details of lying in a crib and thinking, in today's parlance: "This sucks. I want out of here. Sleeping is boring." Later, before school years, I can recall going out in snowshoes with my father, watching him mark trees for cutting or planting, or planning where the cutting would be and where the reforestation would take place.

My mother, meanwhile, continued to harbor this tremendous disdain for all things American. In the early years I remember her talking about how she just hated the house because it wasn't good enough. Then she went on about hating New Hampshire, which also was not good enough. And, as always, there was so much that she disliked about Americans. They didn't have any class, she thought. They didn't know how to talk or eat or think or read. The ketchup bottle on the table was the symbol with which she associated Americans. We'd visit Quebec and my friends there didn't seem to know that I was an American. I myself didn't really quite grasp my nationality for years. I must have been eight or ten before even having it dawn on me that "American" was my identity. That must have a lot to do with being brought up by a French-speaking mother.

When I was five and my sister Louise was born, it reaffirmed my own independence. My mother had been accustomed to living among a well-defined group of relatives and friends. It must've been very anxiety-provoking for her to have had a baby by herself in Michigan without the benefit of any family or emotional support system nearby. My response to that, not uncommon for bright, strong-willed first children, was to become the unneediest little kid a parent could ever want. Through my behavior, I said to my mother in effect: "If this makes you so nervous, then I'll just simply need less and less from you." This, of course, amounts to sort of a preconscious mode of thinking. One response a baby can give to the onset of anxiety in a parent is to become more upset, escalating the perceived need for attention. Another, which is what I did, was to pretend I didn't need the attention—whether it was true or not.

I also remember my mother having a miscarriage, the trauma of which I would come to appreciate personally nearly four decades later. I can recall people running around, with my mother lying on the bed and my physician-uncle giving her injections. My parents wanted at least two kids. Of course, birth-control methods were virtually unknown in those days. Abstention and luck were just about all there was. The pregnancy that led to my sister's birth gave me my initial opportunity to observe and ponder the wonders of the life process. When my sister was born by Caesarean section, I recall seeing her in the arms of my mother and wondering about the miracle—the "miracle" mainly being: How did this formerly enormous pregnant woman get so small again so fast? Such is a child's frank empiricism—or mine, in any case. My conscious memories of my sister are that I thought she was the greatest thing imaginable from the beginning, and our parents say that jibes with my behavior.

Louise was born in April 1953, and that summer I went to Quebec to stay with my grandparents for two weeks. Every summer after that the visit was extended until I was spending the entire summer away from home. My mother would come up for a month, but Louise never stayed the way I did. At the time I suppose I assumed the visits constituted a terrific advantage. After all, what child wouldn't want to go off and be doted on by adoring grandparents for a summer? Looking back, however, there must've been a part of me that felt terribly abandoned during those years. I remember thinking from time to time that I wished my parents and Louise were there— that I wasn't by myself. So it appears as though maybe I wasn't quite as independent emotionally as I tried so hard to be.

There wasn't anything insidious about the vacations with my grandparents. My mother viewed the whole experience as a tremendous enrichment because she'd done the same thing as a child and felt much better for the experience. My French-speaking family members in Quebec were jubilant about having this little American family member in their midst. As far as my grandparents were concerned, I could do whatever I wanted. My dad thought at the time about the potential problems that could result from the separations. In fact, he and I spoke not long ago about those summers and the reality of being separated. I asked him: "Didn't you miss me?" He said of course they did, but he felt the advantages outweighed most of his concerns. Besides, he wasn't really sure if he could or should voice any objections, since the summer visits had become such a venerable part of my mother's family tradition.

I can certainly understand the reticence of my father, who was only trying to do the right thing. Part of what has made me outspoken over the years, however, has been the belief that so many problems are caused by what goes unsaid. I shock a lot of people with my occasional bluntness, but I just don't believe in holding back. Years after coming to this realization, my male peers at med school thought of me as "one of the guys" because they knew they could say anything in front of me and I could do the same with them. For most of them it was the first time they'd ever encountered a woman with whom they could speak and act the way they would with men.

In any case, the summer separation obviously had the advantage of making me feel that I was the special kid in the family. Louise might have been able to join me, but when she was three and old enough for the visits, she contracted a terrible ear infection. "Family" medicine circa 1956 was so insensitive that my three-year-old sister was admitted to a hospital and my parents were told they couldn't see her again until she was ready to be discharged. Not once! She was being given penicillin intramuscularly, and thus quite painfully, every four hours around the clock and yet was effectively kept from her parents in that hospital for three days. My sister understandably was a total wreck in the aftermath. She wouldn't let my mother go, insisted on sleeping with my parents, and clung to my mother's leg all day long.

The treatment of my sister says a lot about the flagrant lack of humanity of medicine as it was practiced relatively recently. The experience also went a long way toward defining sibling roles. My sister became the frail, dependent one as my parents felt exceedingly guilt-ridden about the hospital experience. Louise overcame her dependence. A brilliant woman, she is now an accomplished attorney with degrees from Radcliffe College and Cornell Law School.

My own independence, never in doubt, became even more acute

as my sister claimed a lot of my parents' attention. Did I like this development? Not really. But it was as though I consciously concluded that, since Louise would be the frail one, I'd have to be the strong one. My sister's fragility, however, was accompanied by a fierce temper, and I remember her chasing me into a bathroom and turning purple over some transgression I'd committed.

At about the time my sister came along, I started kindergarten, which was something I adored. It's vague now whether I played the title part in a Goldilocks production or would have preferred to play a bear. During kindergarten, in any case, I was animated and outgoing, loving every minute of the experience.

The idyllic year was in stark contrast to first grade at a school run by nuns. These were a bunch of creatures who seemed in retrospect to have been so many female Darth Vaders. Only their milky faces and hands could be discerned, with nothing else that seemed to the eye of a six-year-old to be identifiable as belonging to a human being. Everything about the school experience was rigid and structured, and I initially dreaded it to the point that I vomited every day between the car and the classroom. The nuns looked forbidding with their vestments, which I originally thought were made of corrugated cardboard, like play costumes. They wore these starched white, round halos around the top, and more starched white stuff hanging down the sides, and another white starched collar that you could tell was making their necks red. At the base of all this was a silver heart with a crown of thorns on it dripping blood, and seven swords. Believe me, you see something like that up close for the first time and you think to yourself: "I'll be more than happy to do whatever they want."

Then there was what the nuns wanted, which was much more rigidity. I'd never been told, for example, that you couldn't go to the bathroom when you needed to, so I had the great good fortune of wetting myself a few times in first grade, adding to the general humiliation that the daily disgorgings had brought to the experience. Someone from the school called after a month and told my parents:

"You've got to make this girl stop vomiting." Evidently I did. It was part of a plan I affected in order to gain favor. The idea was that, if I did exactly as the nuns asked—turned in perfect school work, wasn't "obstinate" in their estimation—then they would be friendlier toward me. Figuring out the way the school rules worked had the effect of settling my anxieties to a point where my autonomic nervous system became controllable again. But despite my outward appearances, I realized that the school work, which was no problem for me, was the only saving grace of early grade school. I prided myself early on in being one of the smart ones, and there was never any doubt about whether I'd go to college some day. The fact that I excelled scholastically saved me during puberty, when it became clear to me that I wasn't magically going to evolve into a slender, "popular" girl in the traditional sense. Many tearful nights during early adolescence ended with the consoling reminder, "Well, at least I'm smart."

Home life was fine during those years, what with television being available after homework. I remember being terrified somehow by Pinky Lee, and for some reason "Hopalong Cassidy" gave me trouble. But I probably watched a minimum of an hour of TV a night, and in so doing was informed, as were most kids of my generation, of "The Mickey Mouse Club," "Zorro," and the rest. There was some kind of censorship imperative at our house, and I could never figure out how my parents always knew I was watching something I wasn't supposed to see. Then I realized that they were tipped off by my attempt at being clandestine, i.e., turning the volume down. I can't imagine what existed in those days that would be bad for kids to watch, especially when compared with what today's kids see on TV.

There was a family with kids of various ages near enough to our home so that my sister and I could play with them, but none of the kids was a girl my age. I don't carry a single friend to this day from grade school, perhaps because of the difficulty of seeing peers on social occasions in an environment that called for commuting fifteen miles to school. In fact, the friends I made at medical school are the only ones with whom I stay in contact. A friend from high school alienated herself during a twenty-year reunion when she greeted the news that I give medical exams to women with an astonished remark about how she could never imagine one woman treating another. I thought: "Okay. There goes that friendship." I said to her: "Well, you know the way it works is that everybody gets to choose these things and, by the way, I think I'll be going to talk with somebody else now."

Today I'd probably let such a remark slide, but in 1986 it was obviously another matter. Now I might say to her: "You know that reluctance to see a woman physician is really interesting. Do you have any idea of why that is?" The answer to such a question often uncovers a fascinating thought process.

My classes during the twelve years at the same school were small by today's standards. The graduating class had about forty students. The day was divided to accommodate half English and half French instruction, much of the latter being Catholic-oriented. To this day, then, religion exists for me only as it can be expressed in French and Latin. We also were taught most of the humanities in French with much of the science curriculum offered in English. Couple this schism with typical left-brain, right-brain differentiation and you wind up with an utterly compartmentalized way of viewing the world. The emphasis on French, in any case, derived from the number of "Canucks" who lived in New Hampshire. The term "Canuck" was intended to be pejorative because it supposedly meant you were backward: some kind of laborer or logger, or you stemmed from a family that had killed animals for a living in the recent past.

Here again, for lack of a clear national identity (I at once was and was not thoroughly American, Canadian, French-speaking, or English-speaking) I consciously chose another personal identity. My total identity became wrapped up in intellectual achievement. There were about five of us who were the "bright ones." The priest would come in at the end of every quarter and hand out the report cards in rank order, and pretty much the same five kids always were the first ones. It was very clear to me how I would define myself: I may not live near town, I may not like being an American, but I'm smart. If I hadn't had that identity to hold onto as I was growing up, I honestly don't know what would have become of me.

As it is, what I became was a waitress.

3

You Could Be a Doctor!

My intellectual achievement brought incredibly high regard from my parents. From very early on it was understood that I'd have to pursue a profession, even if it only meant that my life would have a fall-back position in case the prevailing expectations about marriage and family didn't pan out. These, of course, were society's expectations. It seems odd to note from a 1990s perspective that girls of my formative years were expected—at least through the 1950s—to follow pretty much the same traditional paths most women had walked through the centuries. My own mother, however, always made it very clear that she regretted not being a professional. She never said it outright, but we knew. I have no doubt that under other circumstances or in an era more favorable to women my mother could have handled both kids and career with no trouble at all.

It was pretty clear by my family's consensus that the best professions were medicine, law, and education. The latter was understood as being a college-level educator with a Ph.D. Outside of those three options, though, there really wasn't much else that was considered

41

worth looking at for a life's work. It was with great anticipation of meaningful life's work that I pursued school with such relish. Did I go after academic achievement in a dutiful sense? I think I did it more for myself than to meet parental expectations. In truth, though, I guess I never gave my parents the chance to say it was okay if I wasn't first all the time. Even if they'd said so, I still would have insisted on striving to be valedictorian senior year, straining to be first.

My mother never really had a lot of confidence in herself. Whether that derived from the social differences of her early marriage or the financial hardship into which her family was cast, I'm not sure. In retrospect, women in the fifties generally seemed to lack identities. The mother of a friend of mine was hospitalized frequently for "rest"—I guess it had to do with nervous breakdowns. In those days it wasn't unusual for women to be hospitalized for a month for "nerves." It was never clear to me whether in this case it was for drying out or for true psychiatric illness. What does seem pretty clear in retrospect is that women of that era got little credit for what they did. Their identity was as "Mrs. Joe Blow," and if they were like a lot of women of my mother's generation they actually could be persuaded fairly easily that they didn't have the brains or the talent to do anything outside the home. My mother received that message from her upbringing rather than from the marriage. There wasn't any condescending about sexual roles in my family. We lived in a very unusual household in that my dad would do the vacuuming, make Sunday breakfast, and help with the dishes. This sounds like token domestic effort now but it was extremely liberated for those days.

Not that our household was one of unmitigated domestic bliss. Like most families my parents argued about not having enough money. But such quarrels always seemed to me to be no more than an acceptance of a bad situation, a way of taking things as they were without thinking about doing anything about it. If such a family were truly poor—and I certainly never felt impoverished as a kid—then wouldn't it seem reasonable with two of us in school that the mother might get a job from nine to three? But a part-time job wasn't something considered then by a lot of women, my mother among them. There was, first of all, the palpable admission that a woman's part-time work meant the man—the great patriarchal provider—somehow had failed. Then, of course, there was the fact that, as inequitable as women's pay is in the nineties, it was even worse four decades ago. Maybe there was a lot more for my mother to offer than she realized.

My own belief from a very early age was that if you're smart, then you owe something to the world. You should do something with your talent, and it would be a tragedy if you were to sit on your potential or deny it, refusing for whatever reason to use it.

The talent I perceived to be my strongest was in science. Yet my high-school ambition was the rather idealistic notion of using my foreign-language ability and working as a translator at the United Nations. Moving to New York City and doing simultaneous translation in important world affairs seemed romantic to one who wouldn't actually visit the big city until her senior year of high school; on that occasion I was utterly entranced.

Late in high school I remember first considering a career of some kind in medicine. By then I had really gotten into biology and chemistry, and realized how much I liked both subjects. In time it became apparent that medicine was becoming a career preference, which led to a fairly predictable response from some of my mentors. What I particularly recall is the nuns telling me what a wonderful pursuit it would be because medicine would allow me to become a missionary nursing sister. I had read the Nancy Drew-equivalent series about Cherry Ames, the heroic fictional nurse, and so I thought medicine sounded like something I'd enjoy. But it was my parents who, to their great credit, suggested that I could sure be a nurse. There'd be no problem with that. But guess what, Suzanne? You also could be . . . a doctor! And I suppose I must have thought at the time: You know, they're right. So the next time the nuns reiterated the missionary sister subject, I thought: "What a dumb-ass idea that is." I think the whole realization of living as a missionary was what led me to understand that I was definitely heterosexual. The thought of spending all my days alone with a bunch of nuns, cloistered without any men around, made me want to vomit the way I had during first grade.

There were, of course, a number of other assumptions at my school about girls and their vocational destinies. It was an era when students either worked on a college-bound track or a job-oriented course. That's why I never learned to type in high school: The course curricula were so rigid that there was no crossing over. If I had taken typing I'd have had to submit to the non-college-bound course. So I thought: "No way am I ever taking typing on these terms or I'll wind up in some secretarial pool. Instead I'll just get a great job and that way I'll be able to hire somebody else to do my typing for me."

While it was never an issue in my mind whether I'd go to college, mentors always seemed to be there to urge me on. Such was the case with an eighth-grade teacher who noted my potential. Beyond that, I also remember the nuns being very supportive about me going to college, though of course they would have preferred that it be a Catholic women's school.

Instead, I was accepted at the only place I applied: the University of New Hampshire. It offered a good education that was affordable for me and my parents. That was fortunate since I'd amassed some scholarships, but nothing that amounted to a lot of money. It was convenient, too, since Durham was a mere twenty-five miles from home.

Like many children of the fifties, my politics were bound to change when I got to college. While I'd always heard a very Republican point of view at home, "Republican" really meant more of a fiscal-conservative approach to governance rather than a socially right-wing agenda. What I got from my dad, then, was the party line on business and government matters. My mother never became a U.S. citizen, so she obviously didn't vote in elections. My dad had been four-square for Eisenhower, and I believed as my dad did about politics well into the sixties. When the Vietnam War started I was all for it, though that changed radically at college and led to some horrendous political arguments at home. Dad, who had voted for Nixon in 1960, wouldn't support Goldwater four years later, and gradually his politics changed to the point that he never supported Reagan or Bush, either. He also disliked John Sununu's policies as governor of New Hampshire.

But at home I heard GOP boilerplate all through my formative years. Of course, you don't get politicized at a Catholic school, but I was identified as something of a rebel in high school. The main reason, it now seems astonishing to realize, is that at age sixteen I decided to go to work part-time in town as a waitress at a family-style cafe. That led me to understand for the first time that there wasn't any big problem in talking with strangers. The job was a broadening experience, allowing me to expand my social side and envision a much more secular way of life than I'd observed during all those years of church influence. Getting the job also came to pass about the time that some major changes were taking place in the Catholic church. Women could now enter church without a hat to cover their heads. Suddenly women could go to Mass in just a scarf. Then it was fine to wear a lace doily. Finally they said it was probably okay to go with a tissue on your head. That idea brought me to my feet. I said to some nuns: "Look, I have a real problem. This is supposed to be a sign of respect? Going into church with a piece of dirty tissue on your head?" They obviously didn't like such an impertinent analysis, and they let me know that, as an upper-class student, I was setting a terrible example for the younger kids. I was questioning authority. I was being, God forbid, rebellious. I think it was the priest who put it to me in terms of rebelliousness. Even though I'd actually questioned authority and felt the elation that came with it, I remained cowed by priests and what they represented. My family, after all, went to Mass every Sunday (my dad, going along to get along, had converted to Catholicism), so of course the priest was a dominant person in everyone's life.

Aside from such acts of "rebelliousness," I was the sort of high-school kid my own sons would immediately recognize now as a nerd. Unless and until you got a driver's license there was very little mobility, and about the only social outlet was a greasy French-fry joint. If I went there my mother would smell the evidence on me and rail against the idea of a young woman of a certain social bearing being seen at such a place. It seems so incredibly tame compared with the lives of other kids, past and present. I smoked, but only for about six months during college. Drinking was confined to an occasional celebratory glass of wine or sparkling libation at home. I had a boyfriend for a while, a major attraction being that he was two years older and had a car. My mother's ideas about social standing came into play again, even though the boy's father ran the local furnace-oil company and undoubtedly made a fine living. The relationship, anyway, was based mainly on companionship, with the boy's car providing a private place for necking. I remember lusting after another boy, though I didn't go out with him until he'd moved to Boston and I'd gone to Durham.

I've been asked when the seed, so to speak, leading me to become an abortion doctor might have been sown. The answer is difficult to give, because abortion just wasn't something anybody even thought about. In that environment, premarital intercourse was not even within the realm of possibility for me. Sex seemed so remote to me that the notion of abortion must have seemed light-years more distant. Where high-school girls of the nineties no doubt discuss with one another the contingencies that might lead them to choose abortion, peers of my era never broached such a subject. Nor was it ever discussed in my family. In what context could it possibly have occurred? None. I mean, try to imagine the debate team at a strict Catholic high school taking up: "Resolved: Federally funded abortions shall be provided on demand."

At school there was no lecturing against it because there was little mention of sex to begin with. We had no realistic sexual instruction from the nuns. There were just a couple of vague, virtually useless sex education classes in high school, the boys and girls meeting separately, of course. In our class we talked a little about tampons, and one girl wanted to know whether it was a mortal sin to use them. After all, she said, in order to use a tampon you might have to, you know, touch yourself. I can't remember quite how the answer was phrased, but it turned out tampon use wasn't even considered a venial sin, but merely one of those dreary necessities brought about by the dread progression toward womanhood. Recalling all this from a nineties' vantage point seems as though I'm recalling some repressive girl's school from Victorian England. But in some ways the repressiveness of my formative years must have been worse given the more permissive social and political climate of the time with rock music, the civil rights movement, and emerging radical politics.

At home I guess it was understood that sex was supposed to be a fun thing, though it also was understood that it would occur only in a committed relationship. I was expected to graduate from high school a virgin, and probably from college, too, unless I got engaged. That was the parental expectation, half met, as it turned out. But I just didn't believe all that propaganda from school about how sex was bad for you, because it was clear from my parents' own example that it couldn't be true. It's the sort of healthy example I hope my husband and I pass along to our children as they come of age in the time of AIDS. With that in mind, I recently found myself telling my oldest son that my expectations for him are: graduate from high school, drug-free, nonalcoholic, a nonsmoker, and a virgin, and he shouted: "You mean I can't have sex!" He was okay with all the other requirements, but no sex? C'mon.

But my parents never talked about their birth-control methods. If Mother had already given birth to four kids and gotten pregnant again, the issue might have arisen. But it never did, except in an implicit sense in relationship to menstruation, about which I had a kind of vague idea. My mother told me about it, but I wasn't really sure what was happening to me on that interminable day when the class went on a field trip to see *The Ten Commandments*. This is a very long movie under the best of circumstances, but longer still if you happen to have just started your first period. Let's just say I was very uncomfortable and for a very long time. When I got home I told my parents I had this terrible pain in my abdomen and my mother said: "Well, you're going to have to get used to it, because it happens every month." And then, not long after, when I was up all night moaning and groaning and vomiting with a temperature of 103, my parents thought such symptoms weren't quite what would normally be expected during menstruation. They were correct, of course, and my poor mother carried the guilt of having "caused" my ruptured appendix. In eighth grade, then, I started menstruating, had a ruptured appendix, had surgery, got chicken pox within two weeks of the surgery, then got rubella within three weeks of the chicken pox. So I missed an entire month of school with a veritable medical encyclopedia of afflictions. As an eighth-grader I concluded that all this trauma and setback meant I'd never get into college. I was obsessed, worrying about it all the time. Nobody else at the time thought I should worry. I guess I had always exhibited such confidence that no one could believe I might have doubts about my performance. I'd go to take a test, be particularly nervous about the examination, and hear: "Oh, don't be nervous about it, you'll do fine. You always do." Just once it would have been nice to hear: "Yeah, it's really nerve-wracking to have to take a test, isn't it?"

The truest social feedback, here again, seemed to come from my waitressing experience. I absolutely loved waitressing. It was a way to talk with people and it proved invaluable in that regard. But in a mercenary sense it presented a way to see how much niceness it took to get more tip money out of customers. It also proved to be a great experiment in efficiency. I came to realize that if I could convince those customers that I was still aware of them and cared about them, then they'd wait three times as long for an order to come up. It worked—and works in real life, too. Is there anything worse than having your waitress or waiter keep coming by and ignoring you? So I'd pay special attention to customers when the food wasn't coming up and keep offering something more, something else, and by doing so I'd be able to keep them on my side.

I started working when I was about sixteen. If I was going to be enjoying skiing, horses, and cars, then I'd better start bringing in some of my own money. Both of my parents were committed to establishing a strong work ethic and I loved assuming the responsibility of maintaining a job. My parents asked my sister to do the same when she turned sixteen, but as it happened she hated waitressing—couldn't stand talking with all those strange people. But I kept going, working there until I was old enough to serve wine. That was when I turned twenty-one and finally started to see how you really earned tips: You talked customers into the different kinds of wine that would go with their meals, ran up the tab, and everybody was happier in the bargain.

Becoming sixteen and having mobility and a job and a future meant that all of a sudden life was absolutely wide open. That's when I began to see my life moving in different directions. I'd traveled the road back and forth between the house and Rochester thousands of times, but now it occurred to me that I'd be going well beyond where I'd been. Of course, I still had no idea where that would be. Nearby Durham seemed distant compared with my high-school boundaries. If that were the case, then life beyond college graduation seemed much more distant.

When I was eighteen my parents drove me to college for the first time. My mother remembers it better than I do. I imagine in retrospect that, like most incoming college freshmen, I just wanted to get away and be on my own. Mom always said it was like "bringing my lamb to slaughter," when all I could think of was: "Hey, this is really, really cool." I didn't have the feeling about it that I know will prevail when my kids leave home, which is to say: "This is a major marker in life," "They'll never live at home like this again," and; "We'll never have the same relationship again and there's nothing I can do for them anymore." So maybe my poor parents were going through some of this, while all I could think of was: "Wow, college.

Cool! Your own dorm room, you get to eat out all the time, and no-body's here to tell you what to do."

In fact, the greatest source of continuity with my earlier life from that point on may have been that I always had the waitressing job to go back to. I also, of course, had the gathering awareness of what I eventually would do with this accumulation of education. It was going to be medicine or law: That much had been concluded from my high school years. By then I also knew that if it were to be law then it might mean politics as well. The allure of politics would become greater as I came to greater social awareness in the university environment of the late sixties. Yet, despite what would happen in college with the antiwar movement and how it would help me change and become more outgoing, I managed to stay pretty well grounded in Rochester by working during school vacations back in that family restaurant.

In time I would make the critical decisions that would lead me to the work I do today. Years later it would dawn on me that although it seems that I've worked constantly since age sixteen, in truth I've held just two jobs my entire life. I've been a waitress and a physician, and for a variety of reasons I've loved both of them.

4

The "S" Word

That I was still a virgin at twenty-one both amazed and appalled my young sons when the subject came up during a family hot-tub session one evening. They were amazed because it sounded a little prudish to be starting to experiment with sex so late. One of my sons reacted by saying: "Didn't you have any fun at all?" A little quick math also revealed that my first sexual partner hadn't been their father, whom I hadn't yet met. The whole subject prompted one of those great kid responses, because they had done a good job of setting me up for the revelation to begin with. And when I finally shrugged and said "twenty-one," one of them shouted: "That means you had sex with someone before Dad!"

"Yep," I replied. "That's what it means, all right."

Odd as it may seem with today's sensibilities, I guess I had always just assumed you waited a while to experiment with sex. Freshman year, in any case, I learned a critical lesson about the advantage of checking out your audience before you make pronouncements. In the dorm there were four of us women shooting the bull during one of those frequent, interminable late-night sessions. Two of us were clearly virgins, and the other two we assumed were virgins. So we went on and on about "personal responsibility" this and "emotional attachment" that. Pretty soon we hit on the notion that our parents had been allowed a lot more freedom and had a lot more sexual experience, and then here were the four of us supposedly thoroughly modern young women, with none of us ever having "done it" before. At this point two of the women raised themselves up and said: "Oh, yes, we have." And, naive as it seems now, I thought: here they were, they'd actually had premarital sex and didn't have any of the markings my Catholic, guilt-ridden upbringing might have predicted. They didn't, for example, have hair growing out from under their fingernails. They weren't dissolving in front of me like the Wicked Witch. They didn't have pimples all over their faces. In fact, for having experimented with the "S" word they looked pretty normal.

That appearance of normalcy must have made quite an impression on me. And yet I was still nearly three years from my own initial sexual encounter. I met my college boyfriend and first sex partner during the winter of freshman year, so I wasn't even nineteen yet. Vestiges of my earlier life were such that I still went to Mass every Sunday through sophomore year. In retrospect that seems amazing and incongruous given the other changes taking place in my life, but it all seemed to fit fine back then. At least the priest near campus was a good guy. It was the first time I'd heard anything intellectually stimulating in terms of a sermon. By then the Mass was spoken in English. Attending service was almost like dabbling in philosophy, and since my boyfriend was a Catholic, we'd go together and get something mutually useful out of the experience.

This partner was an extremely nice man, with all kinds of skills and interests that were different from mine. We went together even after I started medical school, and he really wanted us to get married. We somehow managed to remain virginal for more than two years before we had our first sexual experience, an occasion that proved terribly unpleasant for me at least. I lay there and thought: "Shit, this hurts. I hope it isn't going to be like this every time." We'd even bought condoms for the occasion, but didn't use them. I was quite sure I didn't know at what point you were supposed to stop and do "that" with the condoms. The entire procedure seemed somewhat alien, which I guess is the case for most people experimenting for the first time.

But then this man and I developed a wonderful sexual relationship. He and I should both feel grateful to one another because we learned together and seemed to have fun every single time, and the thought of nonmutual orgasms simply didn't exist, which is to say that the thought of one of us having an orgasm and not the other never entered either of our minds. And I'd come to realize from discussions with other women that it was quite unusual to have such a considerate and compatible male partner. He truly viewed me as a life partner and I toyed with the idea of marrying him. I'd set up an almost quantitative analysis, thinking to myself: "Well, he's so good at this, this, and this, but then he can't do this and this." My parents thought he was a very nice man, but they showed that they had no desire to have him as a son-in-law. They felt that the relationship was unequal and that I would "go farther" professionally than he. I remember thinking about why it was you had to struggle with relationships and commitments.

I came to realize that breaking up was inevitable, though that scarcely made it less horrible. I had noticed John, my husband-to-be, the first week of med school, and I thought: "Gee, isn't it nice they let high-school kids come in and see what medical school might be like?" and somebody said: "No, he's in our class." If I had taken a little closer look I might have noticed that John was somewhat more physically mature than high-school kids. He would have had to be, given that he'd been captain of the Harvard football team, not to mention school heavyweight boxing champion. But his face looked extremely boyish and, for that matter, it still does to this day. When I first encountered John I was totally devoted to my boyfriend. But I invited John to my house for a Halloween party, the plan being that perhaps he'd meet one of my roommates. Then as I talked with him, I found him to be a very interesting guy. Later in the year, as we continued getting to know one another, I found myself upset with him because he invited his old girlfriend to the Christmas party instead of me. I guess getting mad for such a reason is a sure sign of blossoming affection. As it happened, it was not long after Christmas that we first dated. It was the sappiest of first dates: we went to see *Love Story*. After that the romance proceeded very rapidly and heatedly, and I soon realized that I was being totally unfair to my old boyfriend. The guy was still writing to me while I was dating John. I'd still see the old boyfriend on occasion and finally it occurred to me I had to be totally direct and honest with him. We met one night and I told him: "You need to understand that there is no hope for our relationship whatsoever. I'm totally taken with this other guy." It was mean and I genuinely regret it, but it also was direct and brought closure to a relationship that couldn't have gone on.

That my first serious thoughts about pursuing medicine had come up in high school, when I took biology and chemistry, proved to me something of an irony when another science course nearly killed my ambition. Early during my undergraduate years I figured if I was going to be in premed then I would do well to take microbiology. It was an utter disaster. I hated that course more than anything with the possible exception of biostatistics in medical school. After the first few sessions of microbiology I threw up my hands and concluded: "Well, I just can't do this. I truly don't care about all those damned little bugs."

I was double-majoring in premed and government at the time, and I thought I'd better keep my options open. By then I was nearly a sophomore and becoming more politically aware. Besides, all the fun, radical people were in political science. The premed students were all really dull and I had a hard time relating to them, but I covered myself and completed all the requirements anyway. But I also finished all the government courses and in fact earned an undergraduate degree in political science.

The University of New Hampshire was relatively small as state schools go. I think we had about seven hundred in our graduating class. I lived in dorms and off-campus, but I did go through rush freshman year with the hope of being accepted by a campus sorority. It turned out to be a great lesson in "don't try to be somebody you're not," because I never got in. Then I found out that none of my friends had gotten in either, and in retrospect it probably was for the best because it forced us to find our own identities rather than simply adopt that of the sorority.

At the same time, however, I went through many dark days of feeling inadequate, ugly, unable to fit in with normal people, and wishing I was totally different. Spending time with my friends and family allowed me to make peace with "my failure": to recognize now that I must have seemed false for trying to be someone I thought the sororities wanted and to let go of feeling shamed because I had been rejected. It was a painful lesson, but necessary for me in learning what some people seem to perceive more easily: that a rejection is just that, and not necessarily a repudiation of one's entire worth.

Knowing what I know now, in any case, I can't imagine how I would have been compatible with sorority formalities at a time when the antiwar movement made all such tradition seem like nonsense. Dormitory life suited me fine, though the rules for dorm living were relatively stringent in 1966. Presumably as a means of trying to assure chastity, men were only allowed in women's dorm rooms twice a year. That typically translated to homecoming weekend and one other time.

By sophomore year I became active in student government, which led to the creation of a faculty-student senate and prompted a lot of antiwar rhetoric. We held war protests and marched through Durham to get the attention of the local folk. But UNH wasn't the kind of campus where you took over a building or occupied faculty offices. Perhaps the highlight of our antiwar involvement came when we had some of the Chicago Seven defendants speak on campus and I moderated a forum. At the time I suppose we seemed quite radical, but we still worked for change within the system. It's a political position that I prefer to this day.

As far as my awareness and embracing of the feminist movement, I was a much later arrival than many of the feminist women I now know and admire. From my college years on I was politically active with growing global concerns, but feminism didn't kick in for me in a big way until I started my residency in Seattle during the mid-seventies. The politicization process posed quite enough distractions for me during my undergraduate years, representing a considerable change for someone who came to college more or less in support of the Vietnam War effort. After a lot of all-night discussions in dorms and coffee houses, though, I came to the conclusion that I'd been had by a government that had been feeding America a line through two administrations. After that there was no looking back to the political naiveté of my youth.

But beyond global awareness were numerous pressing local concerns in those years. At college we were more than happy to be making changes just in such relatively simple matters as dorm rules, hours, and curfews. I viewed myself as an important part of the political system and, naively it seems, hadn't realized the fact that, as a woman, a whole great part of me was being alienated. Looking back at the student-government-reform and war-protest movements, women were kept in roles that reflected far less than leadership status. But I guess I hadn't been paying any attention. I had never felt slighted, possibly because I hadn't pushed myself as a woman. Anyway, there were two political paths from which to choose back then: the extremely radical Students for a Democratic Society (SDS) route or the student-government approach. I chose to be my own type of radical. I was a loud-mouth in student government affairs, welcoming dissident Abbie Hoffman and others at a huge rally attended by thousands. This was right after the Kent State massacre, so the atmosphere obviously was highly charged. The faculty had insisted that if Hoffman and the others came on campus at all, they must not speak during the night. I guess the fear was that under cover of darkness the potential of igniting more violence was greater. This edict upset my sense of fairness. I got up and gave an impassioned oratory: "Since when does freedom of speech end at 5 o'clock at night?"

I'd come to the realization at about age sixteen that not only could I speak well extemporaneously but that I could do it without getting nervous or self-conscious. Maybe it was a gradual process of first speaking to one stranger at the restaurant, then ten in a school group, then hundreds at graduation, and finally thousands on campus. Since then I've had no trouble appearing in TV forums or speaking on the radio. In fact, the audience during my professional years has become anybody who will stand still long enough to hear me. I never, in other words, felt a need to take any assertiveness-training courses. I'm self-taught.

I hasten to add that I was the *vice* president of student government, not the president. Here again, women could go only so far in government at the time—maybe it was a precursor of the Geraldine Ferraro assumption—but it scarcely mattered with all the fun I was having in my senior year. By then I had all my hard courses out of the way, had been accepted at Harvard Medical School, was already Phi Beta Kappa from junior year, was accumulating other honors and titles from student government, and was, in short, a big fish in the small pond of the UNH campus. Senior year was so relatively easy that I was even able to spend a lot of time taking tutorials in horse-back-riding, which prompted me to pursue the recreation as a life-long hobby.

Perhaps my greatest academic satisfaction in my senior year came when I actually scored a recommendation letter to Harvard from the president of UNH. I'd rejected a law career a few years earlier after deciding that, as a woman, I was going to find it much harder gaining acceptance in the legal field than in medicine. It may not have been a well-founded decision at the time, but it was based on inferences I drew from a number of friends and family members. In retrospect I might have found a most fulfilling career in law or a related field. But I also was proceeding at that point from the belief that I had a lot to give back to society and the best way to give back would be as a physician who was also political. By the time I decided to go to medical school, I had my life's plan in place: I would become a family doctor and revolutionize care for poor people.

I applied at medical schools at Tufts University, Boston University (where I was rejected), and the University of Vermont, in addition to Harvard, the latter application not being filed until the final day before deadline. Little did I realize that a rolling-admission policy meant they'd already settled on 50 percent of the class before my application came over the transom. I found out by late winter senior year that I'd been accepted at three of the schools. Knowing as I did that the odds against getting into Harvard had increased because of my late application, I was utterly thrilled with the acceptance, particularly because advisers at UNH had said I shouldn't even have bothered trying to get in. After all, only one UNH student had ever matriculated there and it was a "he," they reminded me. "You can't do it," was the message, "both because you're a New Hampshire graduate and because you're a girl." I thought: "Well, we'll see about that." Not only did I get in, but I got a scholarship. And it wasn't because I was a "girl," either. Sexual tokenism didn't work that way back then, nor does it work that way now, not at Harvard anyway.

Clearing up my immediate future meant I could afford the time, if maybe not much luxury, of a trip to Europe with two women friends during the summer of 1970. Traveling on second-class Eurorail passes and crashing at youth hostels made a Western Europe tour affordable in those days. Even with a partial ride to medical school I would wind up accruing about $8,000 in student loans by the time I finished. It seems amazing that college was as relatively inexpensive then as it was. My debt when I graduated in 1974 seems a pittance compared to the crushing debts owed by current graduates, sometimes as much as $100,000.

The Europe trip was typical of student adventures of the era. My French, and the German spoken by another woman, served us well from Paris to Berlin, which was a pretty forbidding city in those days. Otherwise, we toured wine country and poked around the cathedrals and museums. I was overwhelmed with appreciation of the age and infrastructure of the culture. Just as daunting was the contrast with the relatively brief life span of the American culture. I remember consciously imagining how America would have been nothing but prairie grass at the time when the great European cathedrals were constructed, when the Renaissance paintings and sculpture had reached classical status. I decided that I loved the European way of life: the mode of eating, of sitting in cafés and having conversation. And, upon returning to the United States, I tried not to be struck too deeply by the relative vulgarity of American culture. That's something I've gotten better at over the years (I figure I'm an American and the rest of the world can just deal with it), but during the first couple of trips to Europe as a student I tried desperately to make people not notice I was an American. If they thought in France that I was a Belgian student, that was fine by me. But my accent was just ambiguous enough so that French people knew wherever I went that I wasn't from there. It reminded me somewhat of the French-Canadian-American identity confusion of my youth. Nobody could quite figure out where I belonged. In any case, my traveling companions and I did crazy things: take German cabs out to the country and eat raw steak; take risks with strangers that I know I wouldn't want my own kids to attempt. But it seems that we who came to our maturity during the sixties and seventies enjoyed a much greater freedom to engage in such experiences than will ever be afforded the generations that have come after us.

The idyllic nature of the trip, at any rate, was in stark contrast to the intense shock that would come a month after we returned. I had never had to work very hard academically, so I assumed there would be no unfavorable consequence if I could just apply my normal study habits to medical school. It soon came to pass, though, that for the first time I found myself studying with a dictionary propped open next to the textbooks. I couldn't understand enough of the words to even begin to make sense of the context in which everything was being discussed. The experience was that of having to study in a foreign language.

Students really hit the ground at a sprint in medical school. I started course study right away with biochemistry, and something remarkable happened: I flunked my first biochem quarterly. Flunked! I thought: "I should've gone to law school. This is gonna be too hard." It was quite an awakening for someone who had never come close to flunking anything in her life. So I applied myself to the task. This proved most difficult. The experience was extremely rattling for me. Staying on task required significant lifestyle changes. I convinced myself to look at medical school as representing a level of discipline entirely different from anything I had known. I never flunked another exam. My recollection is that I became a very serious student at that point, but classmates later disputed this. They said that they felt the only reason I was studying in the library, for example, was so that I could go from one area to another bothering everybody.

During the initial struggles in medical school it was to my great advantage that I'd gotten an excellent science foundation at UNH. There had been a terrific biohistology combination, and I had superb professors in organic and inorganic chemistry. By senior year I'd built enough of an academic reputation so that I wasn't always held to the same standards as others. The idea was: "Oh, she'll get an A," though one professor made me rewrite a paper because it wasn't of high enough quality. Then he gave me an A before I did the rewrite, just on the assumption that it would be worthy. At UNH it was simply understood that I would finish in the top five.

While medical school presented the challenge of having to work at a much higher level than in undergraduate years, it also led me to make a conscious choice about achievement. I realized that in order to be among the elite students at this level —the top 10 percent of the graduating class—I'd have to give up too much of what I enjoyed. I just wasn't willing to go that far. While it seemed okay doing well enough to stay in the upper half of the class, for the first time in my life I no longer was obsessed with the idea of school as the be all and end all. The trade-off was a good one, because in the bargain I was able to have a social life.

Cliques at Harvard Medical School were formed strictly on the basis of career direction. There was, among the class of one hundred fifty, the group of "bench" people who were going to get research awards and make the Alpha Omega Alpha honor society. Then there was the group of us called "the normal people," who were high achievers but partied a lot and did other things. It was a group of us that came together on the basis, say, of noting that we carried to class the *Boston Globe* or the *New York Times*. But despite the stratification of student cliques, one fact held then as it no doubt does now: there weren't any laggards at Harvard Medical School. After having come this far academically, nobody was going to screw up.

The only screw-up of any kind that I noticed during the early going at Harvard was the utter lack of regard—contempt, almost—that was generally held for the idea that anybody would pursue a career in family medicine as opposed to one of the many specialties. The bias was such that, if you really wanted to do such a thing with your life, then why go to this great citadel of medical knowledge? Why not go to some offshore institute and get your papers?

But the low status of such a pursuit scarcely diverted my attention from my goal. All it did was reinforce the notion that an integrated family-medicine practice would help lead to the salvation of the planet, and I was damned if the Harvard Medical School establishment was going to dissuade me from such a belief. Of course, it never did.

5

Empowerment

No one at Harvard Medical School admissions would have ever admitted it but there once was, in effect, a working quota for acceptance of minority candidates, and that included women. The total had to add up to between fifteen and twenty people—that's women and minorities. The year I started medical school represented something of a breakthrough in that women were accepted without being labeled for minority status, and minority students were accepted independently of women.

I suppose that the school establishment gradually was becoming more open about the idea of having women students, though there were only about fifteen of us in a class of one hundred fifty. For my part, I was just glad to be there, and I didn't have any qualms about being considered "one of the guys." This phrase, which applied to a few other woman students, meant something beyond mere sexual differences. Being "one of us" meant, for example, being part of group open to the idea of exploring gay issues, which had amounted to a taboo subject prior to our arrival. We were men and women living in shared housing. That was big stuff back then and my horizons expanded just by being in the company of a really progressive group of people.

Yet, at the time my awareness of women's issues—abortion in particular—was limited. I hadn't read Betty Friedan by then, and hadn't really looked at any of the feminist tracts that were proliferating during the early seventies. I guess medical school was such a highly focused pursuit that I just didn't afford myself the time to look up from studying and see the women's political issues that would redefine the social order and change my life. On the other hand, I can look back now and see that I was, in effect, living the feminist revolution that others were writing about. My progress from a sheltered, rural Catholic upbringing to the social radicalism of the Vietnam era was remarkable when compared with the relative progress women had made in America prior to my generation. Though I never consciously articulated it at the time, my lifestyle as much as said: "Why read about it if you can go out and do it?"

Not that women's progress wasn't fraught with obstacles. The world doesn't easily yield to social revolution. During my third year of medical school I finally got a prolonged, real-world taste of what the medical profession of that era thought of women physicians. I completed a three-month clinical rotation in internal medicine at Massachusetts General Hospital, where I was the only woman on the rotation. The only inferences to be drawn from the experience were that (a) women were expected to be stupid and therefore (b) women could be forgiven for not doing the work or (c) would be seen as having not done the work. That was the first time I felt truly assailed by that pervasive attitude of: We're not going to expect you to be smart, we're not going to let you show you're smart, and we're not giving you any credit for the fact that you're here—which we don't like in the first place. The idea was that "you're a woman and you're in the way." It was, in retrospect, precisely what women would experience at every juncture during the next two decades as they presumed to aspire to be firefighters or police officers or professional athletes or—heaven help us—political leaders. When women wanted nothing more than professional equality, the dirty little secret came out. America remained pretty much a "boys only" nation of professionals, and there was little wonder why women of my mother's generation and those who came before her often felt relatively worthless. In my case the "no girls" syndrome was manifested in various ways. Maybe it showed itself when, inexplicably, I wouldn't get positive feedback from supervisors for the work I did with patients I saw in the hospital. Maybe it was being looked at askance for presuming to want to leave at a reasonable hour once in a while or hearing praise heaped on every member of the team—the male members, that is— except me.

But second-class status wasn't just reserved for women care providers. Mass General had several treatment centers, among them the Baker House and the elite Phillips House, the latter where some well-heeled patients stayed for up to a year and got the equivalent of first-class service: wine, good food, and so forth. Medical students were taught to draw blood on all kinds of patients, but never in Baker House and Phillips House. We were only allowed in the lower socioeconomic-strata Bullfinch wards—and then only around the women. The institutional explanation was that because old, sick, poor women had such terrible veins we could learn better with them. One might have asked exactly how did the condition of poverty have a direct correlation to poor veins? But no one actually asked back then. Instead, I initially—and naively—accepted such a premise. Then, as the three-month rotation progressed, it dawned on me that the poorer patients were being consigned to what the hospital hierarchy might conclude (true or not) was a lesser caliber of care. Moreover, it was only the poor women who were being treated to health-care that many would have regarded as second-class. I think more than any other experience during medical school this helped politicize me. It demonstrated that in the real world subtle and not-so-subtle discrimination occurs in the damnedest places: respected hospitals, for example. It, in fact, was not true that we would

just care for the old, poor women because of the supposed educational advantages the experience would provide for us. We were as-
signed these patients because they were the most powerless people
on earth. That being the case, the assumption went, you could go
ahead and do whatever you wanted with them. I thought: "Maybe
it's not just me, Suzanne Poppema, being viewed as second-class or
second-best because I'm a woman. Maybe there's really something
larger and more pervasive and more sinister going on here."

This particular clinical rotation, in any case, represented the
most depressing aspect not only of my training but probably of my
life to that point. I was too depressed to put up much of a fight
against it at the time, but the fight came out when I later put the experience into perspective and realized that I wasn't just a dumb,
miserable failure, though I did get my only medical school C during
that period. I guess since it was my first clinical rotation I also consciously didn't want to rock any boats. Then, as I moved out of it and
into surgery, pediatrics, obstetrics/gynecology (OB/GYN), and the
rest, I started to wonder rhetorically—or facetiously—"How is it
I'm so good again all of a sudden? If I was such a miserable failure at
Mass General but such a success elsewhere, then what conclusion
should I draw?"

Here again, these regimens were so difficult that there wasn't really much time to speculate about anything. Timewise, the clinical
rotations were absolutely back-breaking, and it could take tragic tolls.
Suicides among third-year medical students—and we had one, I'm
afraid, while I was at Harvard—weren't altogether uncommon given
the enormous pressure to succeed. You had to be at work early in the
morning, be up all night, spend the next day there, and then, depending on the rotation, either have one or two nights off. Then you
went back and started all over again. But the notion of "nights off"
wasn't the same as "days off." You still had to be on duty during the
day, so you wound up in effect living on duty. It was incredibly intense, which is scarcely a complaint because all doctors submit to the
same intense training. Fortunately, for most of us the training comes

when we're young enough to be at our peak physical condition. If we had to do it in our forties it's doubtful anybody would survive.

But the rigor goes beyond the merely physical. The part of you that is intellectually curious also is taxed by having to assimilate so many different afflictions and diseases. Then there's the fact that for the first time you're actually going to have something to say about this or that patient's medication. Suddenly, after so many years of schooling and training, it isn't a matter of academic speculation anymore. You're the doctor, and knowing that you are can be totally overwhelming. The procedures performed on patients can be terrifying. On top of it all, the medical student is of course sleep-deprived. But, here again, that's as it's always been and still is. It's a situation that practically begs for antagonism. I absolutely believe that the attitude among the vast majority of professors on the Harvard Medical School faculty was to ask a question not to elicit the right answer but to impress upon medical students just how stupid they were. There are exceptions, of course. But it wasn't until later during my residency in Seattle that it occurred to me professors might actually ask a question just to see what I was thinking. At Harvard, it was ingrained in me that, if I didn't do medicine the Harvard way, then people would die by the thousands. Later, during travels not just here but in Europe and the Third World, it finally occurred to me that medicine could be practiced in other ways without catastrophic results. If you talk to people who started at, say, the University of Washington and later went to Harvard, they'll tell you the exact same thing. It's much more benign and mellow at UW, and much less rigid than Harvard ever intends to be.

Having said all this, I don't regret having gone to Harvard, which is one of the finest educations imaginable—if not exactly custom-fit to what I would eventually do as a physician. There was at least something of a respite at the end in the form of a tutorial at Hammersmith, a London medical center for breast diseases. Those of us who attended learned about breast biopsies, breast exams, and, when we had time to spare, about pubs and ale. It was a great break from what we'd known in Boston in that we took two-month rotations, then traveled for a month.

The most fascinating of my clinical rotations was a sequence about death and dying. It forced me to confront and have conversations with people who were soon to die. This had a profound effect on me, helping establish the foundation both for my success as a family physician and my personal growth as a human being. The realization that people were willing—indeed, needing—to talk about their concerns and knowledge and fears of death was mind-expanding. It taught me that the only real way to know about people is to ask and then leave them room to answer.

I also got a lot out of the surgery sequence, an experience that led me to believe I would have been a fine surgeon. Just as worthwhile was the urology rotation, where I'd been led to believe there would be a lot of men predisposed to baiting feminists. I was conscious of such possibilities because by then I was beginning to wear my "go-ahead-and-make-my-day" feminist attitude a little more conspicuously.

It wasn't until my final year of medical school that I took a harder look at the women's movement. I went on TV with the Boston Women's Health Collective, even though I wasn't a member. The group had just published *Our Bodies, Ourselves*, and I was called upon to comment on the basis of being a woman medical student. I was supposed to address the subject of post-partem depression, but as a fourth-year medical student I couldn't imagine what authority I could bring to the discussion.

The television experience might have amounted to my most radical departure to that point but it seems tame compared with what I had in mind for the medical school establishment. It seems absurd now, but it actually came as a smack in the collective face of the school when I announced to one and all that, having succeeded as a woman student, now I was planning to be a . . . family doctor! Such an ambition immediately and yet again defined me as someone out of step with my superiors' expectations for me. The norm would have been to be a nice girl and go into pediatrics or internal medicine, or even be a pioneer and become a surgeon. But family medicine? At Harvard? The attitude was that it somehow meant you wasted your education. Why the negative attitude about family medicine? Because on the East Coast, family docs at best were (and are) considered bandaid dispensers. The number of students annually out of Harvard Medical School choosing family medicine—five to twelve—has remained roughly unchanged the past twenty years. The vast majority go into internal medicine. In fact, there isn't even a training program at Harvard for true family medicine, a program from which a student can emerge board-certified. There are tracks that can be followed for primary-care practice, but there's still no family medicine.

My political beliefs, however, demanded that family care should be my emphasis. If I were to stay the kind of person I was, who was really trying to remain aware of what was happening in the world economically, politically and socially, and if I wanted to help mitigate global problems on a local scale, then this had to be my choice. Besides, by the time I graduated in 1974, the kind of people I really admired were making the same choice and were opting for this relatively new specialty.

There was another reason, though, and it related directly to my growing feminist awareness, which for a time had me wanting to become an obstetrician/gynecologist, but I couldn't tolerate spending the rest of my career with the kind of people I saw on the OB/GYN track. They made me crazy. I couldn't stand them. On the whole, they didn't like women, didn't understand them, and didn't even have any interest in trying to understand them. Why were they pursuing something to which they couldn't relate? Was it just for the money? I don't know. But it does make sense as the perfect place to position yourself if you're really into power over women. That's the ultimate power: the power to frame the debate about a woman's reproductive capacity.

Meanwhile, all of those whom I considered to be the cool people—politically, intellectually, and socially—were the ones willing to risk it for the family-medicine career. It seemed a perfect fit for me. I figured I could take care of families, do a lot for women as a family doc, and also be surrounded by like-minded colleagues. The decision to pursue such a career placed me at the cusp of a major feminization of medical care and my final year in Boston saw me getting involved with a lot more women's activities.

I made my decision about residency not so much because of location (though the Northwest is a wonderful environment), but largely on the basis of the people I'd be working with at University Hospital in Seattle. I'd also applied for residency in San Francisco, Denver, Minneapolis, and Boston. I'd been to the West Coast just once before, and hadn't seen Seattle until my reconnaissance visit in 1973. Seattle in 1974 was an ideal place to be amid the emerging national awakening among women. Washington State had passed its own version of the Equal Rights Amendment, and Seattle was among the most liberal communities in the country. I got involved with women's collectives in health-care very early, and was actually THE feminist that year in my residency program at the University of Washington. A lot of my colleagues were just as politically liberal as I was, but whenever a women's issue arose you could figure on fifteen heads turning to see what I would say. In character, I never lacked for an opinion or an assertion.

When I arrived in Washington after driving out trans-Canada with my sister, I got my first inkling of the casual civility of Seattle. A third-year resident who would be doing a rotation outside of the city said: "Oh, just live in my apartment until you find a place." The thought of someone just offering a stranger an apartment key on the basis of a common professional bond absolutely blew me away. It was quite apart from what I'd come to expect on the East Coast.

The residency group in particular that started in 1974 was very political. Early on we decided that the family-medicine department should be run as a nonhierarchical organization so that the secretary, for example, would have as much to say at the weekly meetings as anybody else. It was the assumption that the whole idea of bosses and subordinates, leaders and followers was bad news. During the years since then it's become abundantly clear that such an ideal doesn't work. You have to have somebody in charge, even though, as I'll discuss later, the structure at my abortion clinic empowers each worker to have a knowledge of and stake in every phase of what we do. In any case, the "we" back in 1974 included six residents per year, or eighteen students—every one of us a flaming, buck-the-system liberal. We showed tremendous pride in our work. We were forever having to prove how good we were during rotations. The expectation at some hospitals was that, since we were generalists rather than specialists, then we couldn't possibly be any good. But I didn't lack for confidence anymore because I knew that, despite the inferences from that first experience at Massachusetts General, it wasn't "me" creating the problems.

Not long after arriving in Seattle I became a member of a loosely formed women's group, an experience that had a significant effect on me. We sat around going through the whole feminist-awakening process, which in brief is: not having a clue, then getting a clue, then being furious that you allowed yourself to be conned for so long. Finally it's trying to figure out what you're going to do next. The group came together around the tenets of a workbook about women's bodies. A friend and I decided that a group process of consciousness-raising would be good; then others joined to a total of eight to ten at any given meeting. It became a pretty fluid group. We met maybe once a month at different people's houses during the next couple of years. (My husband and I currently belong to a reading group, and there are women in the group who are ten years or more older than I. Every now and then it's interesting watching them discover that they're angry about the same things that angered us twenty years ago in that radical women's collective.) Anyway, the workbook that we used called for us to follow certain exercises. One that had a particular effect on me proceeded from the idea that if several people support another human being then the weight of the person becomes irrelevant. To that end, you'd close your eyes and just fall backward, like a stage fall. Your supporters would be there to catch you: That was the act of faith. And I remember the scary but exhilarating process of letting go and falling and being caught. This simple exercise constituted a major milestone in my life: the fact that I could trust a bunch of people with my eyes closed. That they would be strong and be able to catch me was a major revelation and a significant factor that helped me bond with other women. Perhaps I'd always felt I bonded well with men because they were stronger and provided some kind of protection against what was happening in the world. Then there was this tremendous moment when I realized that it isn't true to suppose that when women get together they'll bicker and backbite, and not help one another. In fact, we're incredibly trustworthy human beings. But we've listened to crap for years—heaven only knows where such assumptions come from— about how mutually untrustworthy we are when we get together. Instead, there was trust and bonding. There was physical exploration. We got into pelvic exams. We looked into all sorts of women's issues that never would have occurred to me. It was a very strengthening, advancing, and politically empowering experience for all of us.

That led me very quickly to becoming involved in the feminist medical community in Seattle, which I'll discuss at greater length in the next chapter. By then I'd read Germaine Greer's *The Female Eunuch*, but I still hadn't exposed myself to some of what would become the classic women's-liberation literature—literature that by then was practically considered holy doctrine among the younger women I knew. What I did read brought nothing but reaffirmation and unbending approval: "Damn straight," was my response.

Meanwhile, medical rotations at UW presented the same mixed blessings as Harvard's had, only this time I had one of my best experiences early on. I did an obstetrics rotation at University Hospital and it was amazing the level of kindness and support I got from all the nurses. There was a sense of common purpose and solidarity, the feeling being: "Wow, we're glad you're here and we want you to do well and we'll help you." Later on, at a rotation at Group Health Hospital, it was Massachusetts General all over again, only this time it was the nurses who were entrenched and intractable. It was a competitive women's thing, I guess. I was coming into a well-established social system, where I was neither a nurse nor one of the regular doctors, and I guess it must have been very upsetting for some who had been there a long time.

Did I have total confidence in what I was doing? Not always. I vividly remember driving to work during the mid seventies, headed for the Veterans Hospital and wondering whether anybody else on the freeway was having the same anxieties: fretting about whether they'd be able to figure everything out and perform well. Years later, by contrast, I remember driving to my family-practice clinic wondering whether anybody on the road could possibly be as pleased as I was about the way their day would unfold.

Those first few months in Seattle also presented the occasion that ultimately would change the course of my career. I was about to meet a doctor named George Denniston who was performing abortions—doing so out of a deep commitment to women's rights and because of his beliefs about the need to prevent the births of unwanted children. The following year also would present my most personal experience with the realities of women's choices and unwanted children. It was, ironically, about the farthest thing from my mind when it happened. Naively, perhaps, it hadn't occurred to me that the time could ever come when I might have to make such choices for myself. But, as I discuss in the next chapter, I did have to make my choice in January 1975.

6

My Own Abortion

The old approach to the practice of medicine had been for a patient to come to a doctor to be cured. The physician was in total control. When I became director of a feminist health organization during the mid seventies, our approach followed what we'd done at the University of Washington (and would adhere to in my subsequent practice). It was the partnership philosophy. Patients were viewed as intelligent people who were listened to. Then, with respect to what the patient had to say, the doctor told her what she knew professionally. The patient then made the treatment decision based on the information I could provide. And if the information wasn't enough then I had to get more. We encouraged questions. We never considered an involved patient to be a threat to our professional authority. Instead it was the patient's rightful expression of concern over what was going on with her own body. The old way had been very direct. The patient paid the doctor to tell her what she had to do to get better. "Take this prescription and go away."

Ours was a feminist approach. It proceeded from the idea that women for too long had been *told* about their bodies rather than *asked*. In some ways this was true of all patients of certain doctors but with female patients it had become institutionalized to condescend and lecture. It was as though the woman's body, particularly her reproductive system, somehow was the common property of society. It would be the agents of that society—the doctors—who would tell rather than ask, and if that wasn't good enough for women, then what? What were the alternatives all those years before women became doctors? It was the advent of women coming into the profession that led to a better understanding of the fact that the patient's needs precede those of the doctor or the system. And, ironically, the doctor who had a lot to do with bringing me a great deal of the way toward this level of sensitivity was a man.

My first encounter with George Denniston came shortly after my obstetrics rotation in late 1974. I'd become involved in the nascent women's health-care movement in Seattle. The women I'd gotten to know early on during my University of Washington residency were extremely political, what with taking unheard of steps such as using lay health-care workers to teach pelvic exams to residents. At about this time I had decided I wanted to acquire greater training in abortion and contraception care than I'd been getting through the normal rotation at Planned Parenthood, which took a very stringent approach to the subject. I was interested in something more open-minded than such strict protocols as: "You can't give out birth-control pills for at least twenty-five reasons, and here they are." I could certainly appreciate what the imperatives were for Planned Parenthood. It was a highly visible national organization, after all, and it had all kinds of people coming in and out of the place and lots of observers looking at the organization as though it were under a microscope.

By then, because of the political meetings I attended, I was becoming interested in international population control as well. It turned out that Dr. Denniston was doing humane and sensitive work in that field. His sensitivity was such that he insisted that the videotaped vasectomy procedures show practitioners' hands the same skin color as the skin of those being treated. He thought it made a tremendous difference if, for example, potential health-care providers in India didn't have to watch yet another white practitioner performing some kind of medical procedure on their people. It really stands out in my memory that someone would be sensitive enough to be so concerned about that. He was also very respectful of women; in fact, he was at the forefront of helping see to it that women had the broadest number of possible choices in birth control. Dr. Denniston was heavily involved in envisioning the favorable ecological consequences of contraception and population control. He was an early advocate of building quality of life by keeping sustainable populations, which put him at a considerable distance from the mainstream of physicians of that era. But the fact that he was considered a maverick by many didn't mean he was viewed in a negative light. I'd say he was more of an idealist, bent on practicing his profession with an eye toward doing his work for the right reason. He was definitely a role model and a mentor, and not just in regard to showing me how to perform abortions. He also was crucial in helping to form my global awareness of women's rights generally and abortion rights in particular, helping me realize how nothing less than the fate of the world could have so much to do with establishing and maintaining those rights.

Dr. Denniston by then already had established himself as a pioneer in the use of better instruments for abortion procedures. These were the days, after all, when just doing a suction procedure was brand-new, "suction" meaning, in effect, vacuuming tissue as opposed to removing it with rigid metal instruments. He'd already patented instruments by the time I met him, which seems remarkable since abortion had only been legal for a couple of years.

Initially I went to Dr. Denniston's clinic on a month-long rotation. After learning how to perform both abortions and vasectomies, I returned frequently to help out with those procedures. Key to the tutorship at Dr. Denniston's clinic was the understanding that we would eschew self-imposed waiting periods and do the procedures the very same day. Our attitude was: We trust women to have already thought very seriously about the abortion and all their alternatives before they come to us, and we respect the decision they make. We would, however, follow such policies as "informed consent" and offer options counseling if the women asked for it, but otherwise we would totally trust them to have made up their own minds. We also determined to be very accessible, making it as easy as possible for women to follow through with the choices they had made. After all, that's really what "prochoice" is supposed to be about. Yet, the notion of quick and easy access to abortions was unusual during the immediate post-*Roe* v. *Wade* days. Unfortunately, it's become unusual again because of state regulation, as we'll discuss in later chapters.

But the same-day approach seemed eminently right to me. My belief was that *of course* women are moral agents and would have thought about their options and decisions before coming here. *Of course* there shouldn't be a rule that you have to (a) have your physical exam, then (b) have all your options counseling by somebody else, and then (c) have to go home and think about it, and then (d) come back another day. We don't call this sort of runaround "intimidation" anymore, though that's precisely what it amounts to. Instead, lawmakers lump all this procedural hoop-jumping together under the label of "informed consent," which is a euphemism for "women can't possibly know what's best for their own bodies so we're going to insist that they sit and listen to what the state thinks they should hear." It's the same mind set I experienced first-hand during the one unfortunate rotation at Harvard: "We don't think you know how to think about this on your own, so (a) we'll help you think about it , and then (b) force you to think about it longer." This is only a degree different from legislating away women's reproductive rights entirely. Back in the old days a woman would have to get the consent of two physicians who would agree that her health would be seriously jeopardized by a continued pregnancy. It ought to occur to authorities who set these standards that rights delayed are, in effect, rights denied. Besides, "prochoice" means that the woman, not the doctor or doctors, decides. It was and is our belief that no restrictions shall be placed on that right. A woman who comes to see us about abortion needn't explain herself or her situation to us. If she wants to end a pregnancy, that's her business, not ours—and certainly not the state's. It never ceases to amaze me to hear the expression: "Abortion on demand." What would the alternative be? Abortion by prayer? By edict? Upon seeking consensus? After groveling? Women *have* thought long and hard about this decision *before* they ever get to my clinic. In fact, most of them have been agonizing for days or even weeks, some to the extent of rescheduling their appointments several times.

In any case, my goal throughout my time in residency and working with Dr. Denniston remained establishing a family practice. I wanted a place that would be available for providing all these services along with other procedures normally associated with such a practice. It would be a full practice, where the choice of what I would do for my patients belonged to the patients themselves. I'd help them with fertility if they wanted to have families. I'd deliver their babies, provide good birth-control methods, and do vasectomies if that's what was going on in their lives, and, finally, perform abortions if asked. So my work with Dr. Denniston was a great way to get a lot of surgical and human experience for when I was in my own practice.

His acquaintanceship also helped in 1977, when my fiancé and I determined to travel the globe, primarily to practice at clinics in developing countries. Dr. Denniston offered to sponsor our travel and establish a network of people we could visit so that we could observe methods in India, Thailand, and other countries. My fiancé's residency was in Denver and both of us would be ready to travel by mid-1977. Prior to that I had become more active in feminist health-care issues. I became volunteer medical director for Aradia, the feminist nonprofit collective whose founding goal was to provide health-care by and for women. At the time there still weren't a lot of female physicians, so Aradia relied on midlevel practitioners and lay health-care workers. The latter were providing certain aspects of care under the supervision of the medical director, which was my role even though I was still completing the third year of residency.

If there were legal or ethical problems with empowering lay women to provide certain services, I didn't see any at the time. It was so new in those days to think about delivering health-care to women in a way that was instructive to them. The idea of showing a woman her own cervix was a huge issue back then. This was definitely cutting-edge medicine for the time, even though Aradia's facilities were extremely rudimentary: hand-built furniture and examining tables that were borrowed from other facilities. It was like operating a MASH unit. We often worked under duress and didn't have a lot of equipment. Early on I encouraged the staff to start offering abortion services. The procedure, calling for local anesthetic, dilatation, and suction, was the same as I have used everywhere. Dr. Denniston himself was responsible for donating a lot of the equipment. Aradia not only grew and flourished, but it exists to this day, albeit in much less primitive form.

Looking back on those years, I have to concede that the main reason everything seeming so exciting and empowering for women had much to do with the self-selection process at Aradia and other institutions. I can look back and say: "It was wonderful, liberating, and we were appreciated." But the women who got involved were predisposed to appreciate what we were trying to do. We were of a common mind on women's issues. There were gatherings of women and health-care workers during which women were taught how to perform pelvic self-exams. In this way, the health-care consumer (the woman) could learn enough about her normal anatomy that she would be informed about when to seek medical care. Women coming to Aradia (or to Dr. Denniston's clinic) were exposed to a whole new way of being treated by physicians. To have a woman physician was absolutely unheard of until then. It was an utter, though obviously quite pleasant, shock to one and all to find that medicine could be practiced this way. It was rewarding to the egos of the young female physicians who were involved in this approach. We saw ourselves as pioneers, and justifiably so. Our early successes emboldened us to keep going, to keep moving, and to try more things.

This also was the first time I'd gotten to know other lifestyles. I'd known some male homosexuals in medical school, but wasn't aware of any women who were gay. But some of the women who were at the forefront of medical change were homosexuals, so interacting with them provided me with a social awakening as well. Now I felt fully formed: I was ready to go out and empower women, to save the world, and make sure they have healthy kids if they want them or no kids if they don't. I was ready to be open to different lifestyles and much more. The potential of family medicine seemed limitless. I had the guiding advantage of having been exposed to the Seattle-style family-medicine approach. We looked at patients as total human beings and included in our view of them such related personal aspects as their financial and social situation, and not just their physical condition. Moreover, we family physicians who have been trained at this institution would go forward and from this day on would never again look at patients as specimens or numbers or as part of a system. No one would refer to "heart attack number 34" but instead to "Ms. So-and-So," whose brother is this and whose kids are going through that and whose parents may have gone through the other thing. Rather than restricting our view of patients to their personal histories, we kept *family* charts. That way, when a patient came to see me, I wouldn't make my diagnosis only in terms of that patient's chart. In my ideal practice I'd also look at the backgrounds of the patients' spouses, children, and other family members. I'd want to know about family life so that I could better approach the problem that warranted the visit. Whether this integrated approach would result in more or less death and suffering, I felt incapable of saying. But as far as practicing medicine in terms of what made me happy and made my patients happy, this would constitute a far better way of doing things. It also, I believe, is much more cost-effective by being prevention-oriented. Beyond all that, it's an immensely fun way to practice medicine. Specialists work on subset problems. Family practitioners work toward making whole families better.

With whole-family care in mind I forged ahead in 1977 on a lengthy world tour. The idea was to see how other cultures approached integrated medical practice. Prior to our departure, John and I worked in an emergency room at an Oregon hospital for the summer in order to make enough money for the trip. By August we were able to set out for the Far East by way of Hawaii. The trip eventually took us to India, where we did a month-long rotation that had been prearranged. John made in-hospital rounds while I made rounds in the villages with a family-planning physician who was a Scottish hematologist and an amazing woman. She helped give me an international picture of women and population, but I also saw firsthand a lot of what would help form my world view.

The Punjab, where we were, historically has been a part of India where people are very well fed. Yet families would deliberately starve little girls. You'd invariably see in large families a couple of little girls with reddish, strawlike hair and big bellies, because they were not being fed. They were considered drags on the family. We spent a lot of time going around measuring skin folds and bellies, and insisting to parents: "Feed this baby, feed her." Culturally if you have sons, then they bring daughters-in-law to come and work, and they help in the fields and the family stays prosperous. If you have daughters, then there's the expense of the wedding without the benefit of adding workers to the family. Historically that meant actually killing girl babies at birth. During British rule an effort was made to cut down on infanticide. As a result, families in effect said: "Okay, we won't kill the little girls anymore, but we won't feed them, either."

So the women's lot was as follows: day after day they would go out with the cows and gather the cow patties used for fuel, then do a little bit of gardening, move the cows around, then return home, and cook and try to take care of families. While the mother was away little girls age six and seven were in charge of all their tiny siblings.

What American technology had taught the Indian women was that they no longer had to breast-feed. They could leave the babies home with the other children and bottle-feed them with these fancy new formulas. This was fine, except that then you'd see flies all over the babies' faces, covering the bottles and the nipples, and you knew as a result they would get sick and die. Given a high mortality rate from disease, it made it difficult even to broach the subject of birth control with Indian parents.

So even though I considered myself a fairly worldly person going into India, this was all quite an eye-opener for me. In fact, it occurred to me earlier in the trip that I hadn't even begun to experience anything that would qualify me as worldly. That happened, I guess, when I finally conceded that there was no one to blame for the way things were in India. It would have been more convenient and much less frustrating had there been a focal point for anger. But I found that I somehow was able to stop being angry, and even stop blaming families for starving their babies, after I came to understand the social, political, economic, and historical context in which the conditions exist. Once you understand, there isn't any reason to be angry at them anymore. But it was still frustrating because I knew I wouldn't be there long enough to make a bit of difference.

It also obviously gave me a broadened sphere of influence for perceiving women's problems. Here in the West we sometimes think we've got it bad, but look at what these women are going through. The squalor and utter desperation of Calcutta was a vivid image of what I imagined fifteenth-century London might have been like for the poorest of the population. I was unable to bring myself emotionally to take photographs depicting that level of human suffering: the ubiquitous crush of people, the dying people in the streets, the infestations, kids begging, lepers in various stages of disfigurement—this with my own knowledge that modern treatment is such that there's no reason for lepers to have any physical abnormality at all. People died of tetanus there, a completely curable condition. Now they're starting to teach the lay practitioners in the communities of

India a different system of treatment, and modern treatment methods can put these people way ahead of where health-care had been there. The ideal would be reallocating the money spent on, say, just one jet plane. With that money alone all the eye disease and all the tetanus in India could be eliminated.

Then again, I came to appreciate during that trip just how much a health-care provider has to look at the total context of a patient's life and environment. In Thailand, for example, it just so happened that needles were very highly regarded. As a result, immunization became much less problematic. Moreover, the idea of being able to avoid having babies by virtue of using the birth-control technology that needles could bring met with little resistance. It also was a convenient means of birth control because you merely had to have the provider come through the village every few months and give injections. You didn't have to worry about birth-control pills getting eaten by goats. Moreover, you didn't have to go to a male physician and have an IUD implanted, which is especially important in Thailand, where women find it odious to submit to pelvic exams and treatments performed by males. Once again, then, I became impressed with the fact that the physician needs to make decisions based largely on the broader context of the patient's life.

Then there was the futility of being helpless due to the lack of proper equipment. At one point we were in the north of Thailand making rounds with an internist when she took us to a patient who died before our eyes. The patient had nine-month-old twins and had contracted cholera. Without intravenous fluids or a drip, all of our fancy Western medical education could do nothing for the woman. With needles and IV drips we'd have saved her life.

After a month in Thailand we went to yet more remote regions of Southeast Asia. We found medical surprises in the unlikeliest of places. In Nepal, for example, we encountered a man who was an incredible vasectomy practitioner. He could perform a vasectomy faster than anybody I've ever seen, and seemed to have done so on much of the male population. Was there coercion on his part in order to achieve population control? We weren't there long enough to tell, though it was true that the men seemed willing and the provider seemed nice enough. For our purposes, here again, the visit was an opportunity to observe yet another piece of the international population-control effort, an effort that extends to areas Americans perceive as "the last place on earth." In some ways, Nepal of that era fit the description. While hiking in a remote area one day we met a man who had never seen his face in a mirror, had some vague notion of a king somewhere, had never heard of the United States, and couldn't make any sense of the great silver birds that sometimes roared by above him. And, yes, his ignorance seemed quite blissful.

We were in Afghanistan in the dead of winter in 1978, just prior to the Soviet invasion. I met a wonderful female physician in Kabul, and I assume she and some other patriots we met are long since dead if they weren't able to get out of the country. Given their political views, my assumption is that the Soviets wouldn't have had much use for them. We left for Iran, which also was about to collapse into crisis with the fall of the shah. We weren't privy, of course, to the impending fate of the shah, but there was movement afoot that suggested an American probably didn't want to venture alone too deeply into the country. There was demonstrable anti-American sentiment even then. In any case, I didn't pick up on any sense of women being oppressed because outwardly they appeared to be reasonably well-off. They wore regular clothes and drove cars, and there were women professionals all over the place. We had a good base of support in Teheran because we were visiting friends with whom we had worked in India. Our travels later took us to Israel, Egypt and Kenya before we ended the tour with some rest and relaxation in Western Europe.

If Indian women seemed to have the worst lot among the countries we visited, there also was the pervasive sense—except in Iran— that women everywhere didn't seem to want anything better. They seemed to share an institutionalized sense of resignation in a hopelessly patriarchal world. It was the kind of patriarchy that I imagined the growing antichoice chorus back home had as its ultimate goal. If the reproductive rights of women in America could be taken away, then soon other rights could be denied on the basis of sex. Then it would be only a matter of degree between the girl-starving sensibility of the Punjab countryside and the subjugation of women in our own, supposedly advanced country.

I made an attempt while in Afghanistan to assimilate what literally is the physical restriction of women imposed by the garment called the chador. It presents the equivalent of a horse wearing blinders, but it's worse than that. It's like putting a bag over the body, with tiny openings for sight lines that impede peripheral vision. It's an utter denial of the body. This is the most constricting item of clothing imaginable, yet entire populations of women wear the chador as a matter of cultural imperative. A lot of women in Iran wore it, though not so much in the cities, and women in Egypt, of course, were all covered up. There was a whole culture of women claiming to feel safe under the chador, but my question is: Why do women have to hide under a bag in order to feel safe? Can't women look like themselves? Why is it the women's problem? Isn't it really the men's problem? And what is the proper response in the West to the subjugation of women in other countries? In my view such treatment amounts to an ongoing human-rights violation whose only justification is history and tradition.

When we got back to the United States after nine months of travel my resolve was redoubled to open a family-care clinic. There were a couple of pressing priorities, however, not the least of which was getting married in New Hampshire and lining up jobs in Denver starting in July 1978. The world travel had left me with a tremendous personal need to devote myself to an underserved population. To that end, I worked for the city and county of Denver in Hispanic clinics. It was there that I observed yet again that larger social problems affecting health-care scarcely are the sole province of the developing world. At the time the clinics were broken up into specialization areas so that it was impossible to practice integrated family medicine. This made it clear to me that I needed to go back and do the family-chart method so that I could, for example, observe that a child with a chronic ear infection might have related things going on in the family. The lack of integrated, "one-stop" care during the Denver experience also meant I couldn't deliver the babies of patients I saw or perform surgeries. So I strengthened my resolve to go where I could do things my way.

Some women and I also opened an abortion clinic in Denver after begging and borrowing money and equipment. At the time there weren't any out-of-hospital abortion facilities available—no good clinics like the ones in Seattle. Speaking of Seattle, John and I were finalizing plans during late 1978 and early 1979 to return to the Northwest, where John already had determined to join a practice with some colleagues.

In November of 1978 I became pregnant and would miscarry in January. I thought I would miscarry at home because I was so calm and knew so much about what was happening with me. Then I started to hemorrhage, and initially I was able to distance myself from what was happening by trying to maintain very clinical thinking about the process, i.e., clot size and frequency, cramping, etc. When it became clear to me that my understanding the process wasn't preventing me from hemorrhaging, I panicked. I had waited too long to call for help, once again trying to be an "unneedy" person, and I was terrified. I was actually fainting by the time I called John, which obviously meant I had waited much longer than was prudent.

Did the miscarriage have to do with what had happened in Seattle nearly four years before? Four years earlier I had terminated an unplanned pregnancy and I now, in my panic, was haunted by thoughts of "justice being served," even though I knew the two events were not connected. Intellectually I knew there was no connection. But the fact that I had even a passing thought of "one for the gods" (my polytheistic way of believing I had interfered with the life process once, now it was the "gods' " turn) has made me able to understand and share some of the guilt my patients bear and has helped me to offer them alternative ways of looking at their individual situations. At the time when I chose to abort my pregnancy, I was an intern. I never expected to have firsthand knowledge of the work that would one day be my calling.

Mine was an elective second-trimester abortion. The physician who performed the abortion very easily could have said to me: "You're right in feeling stupid and humiliated. You should have known and should have done something earlier about this." Instead, he was very thoughtful and kind. Knowing I was a doctor, he tried to place the situation in a professional perspective. He told me that this would be a very important, instructive experience for me and for this reason he hoped I would emerge a better physician.

Was abortion the right decision? Absolutely. It was the wrong time for a pregnancy; there was no place then for a baby in my life. I understood the desperation of women who say: "I've got to *not* be pregnant now." For me, it was an excellent decision. When I finally realized I was pregnant, I was absolutely overwhelmed with guilt and fear, and my only clear thought was that I needed to find a way out of this situation. I could see my career plans crashing at my feet. I was terrified at the thought of being a single mother, especially given the fact that I had always believed that having two parents is the best way to grow up. I had no emotional connection at all to the young man with whom I had become pregnant, nor did I desire one. I also know myself well enough to know that if I carried the fetus to term and saw it out of my body as an individual with such a strong tie to me, I'd never be able to consider adoption. I was so desperate that the length of my pregnancy seemed less significant to me than my overwhelming need to end this pregnancy. Having a delivery at five months makes you infinitely less judgmental about how women happen to get pregnant and how they find out about their pregnancy. It made me even more of an advocate for women's rights. I am not a stupid woman and I am not malicious. Yet I was absolutely unaware of the pregnancy. I had completely repressed the thought that my sexual experience had caused the pregnancy. Denial is an amazing human mechanism.

So people come to see me now, shouting: "Why did she wait? How could she not have known she was pregnant?" I can tell them candidly: "Well, you know there are trained, intellectual and very bright women who have denied pregnancies for a long, long time." It's not humiliating, but it's very humbling.

There are a lot of ways people deal with abortions. I recall vividly how I dealt with mine. Since my fetus was at twenty weeks, I could actually feel the fetal convulsions not long after I was given the saline injection. The embryo dies and then I was supposed to deliver, presumably the next day, though in my case it was two days later. A friend drove me to the clinic for the saline injection and later we returned for the delivery, but I never saw the embryo. It happened on my mother's birthday, which I've always found odd. I remember having a special kind of conversation with the embryo at the time: "I'm very sorry that this is happening to you, but there's just no way that you can come into existence right now." It was so clear to me that I was doing the right thing. I've never once had a thought about what that child would have been like now. Whether this is a form of denial and I really did have second thoughts, I can't say. All I know is that I dealt with my grief the best way I knew how. I now relive my own thoughts those many years ago as I help other women on their way to healing after an abortion. I haven't had any second thoughts. I feel absolutely at peace. Such was the case when, after a January 1979 miscarriage and one normal menstrual period, I became pregnant in March and delivered my first son in November.

Part Two

Working

7

The Hippie Doctors

I was one of those lucky people who seem to be able to get pregnant more or less on demand. That was fortunate in the early spring of 1979 because John and I realized that if we wanted a family we had to start soon. I needed to get a practice going and John had his own career waiting for him in the Northwest. Besides, we were in our early thirties and to be trite, we could hear the ticking of our biological clocks. We wanted children and we shared the conscious desire to plan for them. This also was actually a good time in our "doctor" lives to become pregnant. The terrible stresses of residency were behind us and since it was early in our private practices, we actually had more time to devote to being new parents than we would later on as we became busier.

I sympathize enormously with people who have to struggle to conceive. I don't know what John and I would have done if it had taken me several months to become pregnant. As it happens both of our children were conceived and delivered (albeit, quite late in both cases) according to the plan we'd chosen to follow. The timing of the first pregnancy was particularly fortunate considering everything we were trying to do in mid-1979. In order to get the downpayment on a house in Seattle, John commuted from Denver to Peoria, Illinois, where he worked every other week in an emergency room. I remained at the Denver clinics and continued performing abortions at the clinic I'd helped open. In late summer we budgeted just one weekend to find a place to live in Seattle. In later years we would come to realize that it was an ideal home for us, but in our haste to find the place on our trip out from Denver, we got lost. It must have been quite a spectacle, what with cats and a pregnant woman roaming around Seattle in a rental truck, unable to find the house.

It became clear while I was in Denver contemplating my future that I didn't want to open a practice by myself right away in Seattle. It would be better all the way around if I could bond with an established place and then go from there. So I needed to be in the Northwest making contact again with people I'd known during my residency at University Hospital. One advantage favoring Snohomish County, north of Seattle, was that family-care practice already was widely accepted not only by the less urban-oriented public but also by the hospitals, where family-practice physicians had a lot of political power. On the other hand, when I was appointed to the medical staffs at the two hospitals in Everett in January 1980, there were exactly three other female physicians with similar admitting privileges there. Only one of the women was in family practice. While the lack of women was glaringly conspicuous, I was willing to charge ahead anyway. I looked at several practices, eventually choosing one in North Creek, a community south of Everett. The practice, run by two men who were likeminded politically and medically, also held the advantage of being relatively small and fairly close to where I lived in Edmonds.

John joined his practice in September 1979, our first son was born in November 1979 and I started work in January 1980. Not only was our domestic life hectic, but we also were strained from a financial standpoint. In that first year we began paying for a house, buying into professional practices, and would soon be paying for a share of the land on which my clinic sat. All of this presented a nearly unbearable load of outstanding loans. We shopped for bargains at the grocery store and, like everyone else, we counted our discount coupons. Some rooms in our house had no furniture but we didn't mind. Both John and I come from fairly frugal backgrounds and we could appreciate the advantages of looking past immediate sacrifices and toward a better future.

The process of buying into existing medical practices is unfamiliar to most people outside of the profession. First, a new physician agrees to join a practice and is placed on salary for a year. At the end of the year the current partners in the clinic decide whether they want the new physician to join them in their practice, and if so then the recent hire has to decide whether to stay and pay the fee to become a partner or leave. I worked a maximum of five hours per shift, three days a week at the beginning so I could spend as much time as possible at home with our son and still keep up with the momentum of my career. The momentum probably would have taken care of itself, since at the time there was an unmet need for female family-practice physicians in that area. The demand came mainly from female patients, who were absolutely thrilled to be able to see a family doctor who was a woman. "Thrilled," of course, is a conclusion based on anecdotal evidence. Obviously women who would have preferred for years to have had the opportunity to be cared for by another woman were the ones who sought me out and responded so positively. The ones who may have believed, like my former high-school acquaintance, that women attending women was somehow a peculiar concept simply didn't come to the practice. I would have been willing then as I am now to grant anybody the right to feel that women attending women is a bit odd, providing they also believe in a similar aberration in the case of men treating men.

It was, in any case, tremendously encouraging to see my practice grow so fast. When I was working in Denver there were actually days when the patient load was so light that I could steal time to read now and then. With that in mind, I started taking reading material such as medical journals and nonrelated literature to the North Creek practice. But during my first week at North Creek I realized that there wouldn't be any time for outside reading; the initial overflow of appointments soon led to the development of my own core group of patients. A family practice generally draws patients by word of mouth, and evidently people appreciated the fact that we weren't simply processing large numbers of cases. We wanted to take time to talk with people, teach them about preventive medicine, keep good charts, and recognize that a family's health was influenced by what was going on with every family member. My partners and I were of one mind in our desire to take into account total family medical history. Unbeknownst to me at the time, some in the community had dubbed us "the hippy doctors of south Everett." This must have had to do with some of our then-radical ideas—concepts that are much more accepted now. We believed in ideas such as: Women ought to be partners in obstetrical care; the partners of women should be present during deliveries; there shouldn't be a lot of drugs used during deliveries; and, when possible, Lamaze breathing methods ought to be used. Possibly it was our assertiveness that led to us being viewed as different. We asserted with great confidence that, yes, we were the ones who knew the right and wrong ways about childbirth, breast-feeding, and the like. No doubt this was enough in itself to be branded relatively radical, because none of us looked outwardly to be counterculture in any way. Certainly whatever "hippy" inclinations any of us may have harbored had long since past.

This was what was unusual in 1980: We actually asked a woman *how she felt* about being pregnant before ever going on to any other pertinent questions. Before that the approach toward women had been: "Oh, you're going to have a baby! How nice!" Women were told rather than asked. We asked first, then chose an approach to the pregnancy based on what the woman told us. Then we'd talk about her expectations of having a baby and make sure she was healthy from the start. We'd discuss what pregnancy is about and review the standard material on prenatal care: don't smoke, limit alcohol consumption, be aware of dangerous activities. Women would be informed that, while pregnancy carries a lot of risks, it isn't an illness. Therefore, the healthier you are in normal life, the easier you can expect health matters to be during pregnancy. Keep up your exercise, stay active, don't swoon and lie down all the time waiting for the baby to come as Victorian heroines seemed to do. Perhaps swooning had been part of some expectation—even part of a romantic ideal—of the past. But it obviously wasn't a healthy way to proceed through pregnancy.

We would go on to remind women that this was going to be one of the most important experiences in *their* lives and that consequently *they* had a lot to say about how it was going to happen. This was yet another departure from the past, since for years most of the attention in pregnancy was focused not on the woman and her experience but on the end result. Speaking of which, we'd go over a specific "birth plan," discussing it item by item and saying: "Yeah, this will work fine," or "Gee, I don't feel comfortable doing this, but how do you feel about alternatives A, B, or C?" The "birth plan" was a consumer-movement document in which a pregnant woman and her partner would write down in contract form the conditions under which they would like to have their baby's delivery. These requests included low lights, music, the number of support people in the delivery room, medications or not, continuous monitoring of the fetus or not, and use of the delivery room or birthing room. That kind of negotiating was similarly unheard of at the time. Were we less attentive than past doctors? On the contrary. We drew the line at several junctures. I wasn't at all comfortable, for example, when a patient wanted to deliver at home or refused for medically unjustifiable reasons to have an IV or certain medications administered. But instead of insisting on imposing our will as the doctors we would agree to discuss these matters and try to reach a compromise.

By having expectant mothers actually write birth plans, it told us a lot about what they expected, what they didn't know, and what we needed to teach. On the whole, my patients seemed eminently well-informed, and I encountered relatively few of what I'd call off-the-wall birth plans. Those who insisted on home-birthing were informed that I was aware babies could be born safely in the hands of good, qualified midwives. On the other hand, while I couldn't fault them if that's really what they wanted to do, I had to tell them that my hospital-based experience and training had revealed enough unforeseen situations that I'd feel bad if a similar difficulty happened during a home birth. This being the case, I let them know that I just couldn't do home-birthing for them.

By then, of course, I'd had firsthand experience in childbirth, miscarriage, and abortion. I also had been counseled by colleagues on the matter of my son's birth. I remember wanting to discuss whether I needed to have the delivery monitored by a special machine instead of intermittently by a labor RN, and was told by a contemporary physician that I would be risking my baby's life if I followed my preference and insisted on *not* having labor electronically monitored. One of my objections to the monitoring procedure is that it means you're stuck to the bed and you can't move around very freely. The advantage is supposed to be that the monitoring can pick up a field of stress in the fetus early enough so that something can be done about it. My argument then and now is that there's never been any good evidence to show that this is true. In fact, papers keep coming out stating that we can't document the notion that internal monitoring of a pregnant woman in labor has any major benefit except that it makes all the staff members feel better and lets them off the hook, so to speak, in the event of a bad birth. It was just amazing to be a pregnant, strong-willed woman, and a physician, and probably better informed on the subject, and yet be told by another doctor: "That's a stupid thing to do. You'll hurt your baby if you don't submit to monitoring."

Name-calling and condescension were approaches we never used at the North Creek clinic. Instead we'd say: "You obviously get to call the shots anyway you want. I will tell you why I think this or that needs to be done. If we can't agree, then I'll have to decide whether I can live with your decision or whether I need to direct you to somebody else." But it never occurred to me to tell a woman that she was stupid or that the results of her decision were going to hurt her fetus. The importance, rather, was that women were the ones who were supposed to make those decisions for themselves. In various cultures, when left to make their own decisions, women have been doing it really well for thousands of years. All I could see was that a lot of interference from physicians had produced some benefits and a lot of disadvantages.

This kind of talk shocked people, especially when rumors got out about what we were doing. It became public knowledge that we were allowing what appeared to be crowds in the delivery room. Then there were women saying they didn't even want to go to a delivery room, which was another big shock. It was considered radical that I would tell a nurse: "I don't want to hand you this baby just yet. There's a better place for it—with the mother." It soon occurred to me if I didn't cut the umbilical cord, then the nurses physically couldn't take the baby away from the mother right after birth. "But," they'd protest, "the baby will get cold." I'd then remind them: "No, we're putting the baby right on the mom's very warm belly. It's warm because she's been working really hard, and there'll be warm blankets over the top. The baby's not going to get cold." And we stopped doing episiotomies (a large cut made with scissors through the bottom of the woman's vaginal opening to hasten delivery), which also upset some health workers. Sometimes we actually sang songs in the delivery room. It became a joyous family affair to give birth to a wanted child. Afterward women really felt that they had had a lot to say about what happened with them. As much as any patient can feel that she is in control while in labor—which admittedly isn't much—she at least knew that what she said would be listened to. Yet, I never once had a woman argue during an emergency about what we decided to do. I believe there was no protest because the groundwork for the confidence had been set by being with that family for a number of months.

There also were the occasions when women would come to see me because they wanted abortions. I provided abortions for my patients from the moment I started at the North Creek clinic. Did I rush to suggest the abortion alternative? Quite the contrary. If a woman expressed uncertainty about wanting a baby, I would tell her: "There are several things you can do. You can continue the pregnancy to term and become a parent; you can go to term and give the baby to someone else to raise; or you can terminate the pregnancy up to twenty-four weeks, though a termination during the first trimester is preferable. I'm available to help you do all those things. If you're not really certain, then maybe what you need to think about is what it means to be pregnant, what it means to your relationship, your financial life, and other aspects of your life. Spend time thinking about it. You're X number of days pregnant now and you have at least X number of days or weeks before I could arrange to perform an abortion. I can help you with whatever you decide." Some would immediately opt for abortion. I couldn't necessarily do the procedure immediately because it usually meant scheduling time in our surgery room. So we had what amounted to a minimum twenty-four-hour waiting period if only because of scheduling imperatives.

That the procedure would be done on the premises of our practice was of utmost importance to me. I believe that the best way to provide an abortion is having it done not by a stranger but by a family physician dedicated to women's reproductive rights, politically aware of what's going on, and skilled at the procedure. In this way, I found that women weren't frightened when they came to the office. They knew how I felt about them, they were familiar with me personally, and they knew of my philosophies. They were comfortable enough so that the procedure, while not entirely painless, required less medication than might otherwise have been called for.

On the other hand, North Creek being a family practice meant that performing abortions was definitely not my primary concern. We saw people of both sexes and every age. We performed vasectomies, skin biopsies, lump removals—virtually every procedure that can be done in a clinic. We always took care of our own patients in the hospitals. It was an extremely full practice, always busy and always alive with familiar faces. In one memorable instance I started seeing the patriarch of a well-known family, then his wife and eventually his daughter. She got married and her husband became a patient. They delivered a baby in what became one of the most difficult resuscitations I've ever had to perform. The whole family was there—all of them my patients—and the pressure couldn't have been more pronounced. Here I was afraid I was going to lose this baby and I knew how horrible I would feel if it happened. Then again the experience was all the more rewarding when we didn't lose the baby. Various family members and I talked about that delivery for years. The child must just about be in high school by now.

I'd typically see twenty to twenty-eight patients a day. This is down from forty at some clinics, while most family practices see thirty to forty a day. Given the demand by word of mouth, each of the clinic physicians could have seen fifty patients a day. It wasn't as though we ever had any down time. It was just that we afforded all the time we could give to the patients. Quantifying a family physician's patient load is difficult because some people you see frequently and others only come in every five years. I must have seen thousands, though I've never really added up the numbers. Some physicians may think about little else but the numbers, but I never really did. All I could think of at the time was that I loved the work and that it met and exceeded all I'd hoped for while at Harvard. I'd gotten what I felt was a terrific scientific background in school, so I was good at diagnosis. Then I'd learned a lot about dealing with patients during residencies. Applying both skills was very rewarding.

One of the partners at the practice moved on fairly early. I think he may have felt I was more of a radical prochoice feminist than he'd bargained. Then again, he was ready to make another career move. The other physician and I stayed together until we sold the practice. I decided after my first three months that I wanted to become a partner and buy in, which is just what the phrase implies. The incoming physician essentially is paying for the privilege of having walked into a practice where all the equipment has been purchased and the staff is established and trained. Everything exists fully formed, including, to an extent, the patients. This obviously is a tremendous advantage to a starting physician. From a practical standpoint, the new person also buys a percentage of the accounts receivable, which then creates cash flow.

John and I and the baby also were set up well domestically after the first hard year of making so many new adjustments. The baby went to day care and time conflicts, when they arose, seemed to occur during the evenings. Occasionally I'd get called in for a delivery on a night when John was on call. I'd bundle up the baby, call John and leave a message for him to meet me in the emergency room, rush in, hand the baby to John, rush up and do the delivery, which could take anywhere from fifteen minutes to five hours, and then grab the baby from John and drive home again. It was pretty wild, but it worked out somehow. I think this happened maybe ten times during the year and a half that we worked that schedule. You do what has to be done. Who knows? Maybe all that exposure to hospitals will result in our son becoming a doctor some day—though we're not pushing him. Fortunately, in any case, the baby had a wonderful day-care provider. Either our instincts were good or we were lucky because great day-care situations don't happen for everybody. By the time I was toward the end of my second pregnancy in spring of 1982, we hired a live-in day-care person. My second child arrived nearly as late as the first had been: due May 1, he was born May 17—and this after two unsuccessful attempts to induce labor. Finally the third attempt succeeded.

By the time John and I had been lucky enough to have the two children we planned, I also realized how fortunate I was that the practice had proceeded as well as it had. Part of what I'd hoped to accomplish went beyond traditional medical care. I felt that if I could teach women more about their own bodies, then my work would have a cumulative effect that might reach beyond one generation: Well-informed women, that is, would be able to pass along what they'd learned to the next generation of women. In that way, not only would women be better off, but society in general would benefit. True enough, I was able to conclude after just a few years that I had accomplished an incredible amount in the way of educating women, seemingly thousands of whom I'd met through the clinic. It was gratifying that I had also accomplished a lot for the pro-choice movement. While I wasn't yet doing abortions for other doctors' patients, the availability of that procedure provided access to my practice. If a woman wanted an abortion and wished for me to perform the procedure, then she also could become my patient for other treatment, and many did.

But within a matter of a year or so I would begin to take on a number of responsibilities outside the clinic. Still in the first few years of starting a family, the combined stress and strain of trying to do too much with too little time would take a considerable toll. I would become the adviser to a major medical-political foundation, leading to a lot more speaking opportunities and a much greater public persona than I'd had in the past. More important in terms of bringing me to where I am today, I would more or less inherit an abortion clinic. After that happened the weight of my commitments eventually led me through the final stage of evolution to what I am now: an abortion doctor.

8

The Wanted Child

In my opinion the brain of a professional woman having babies doesn't return to full capacity until her youngest child turns age three. Why this is, I have no idea, although I have kiddingly proposed such a thing as a Placental Steal Syndrome. All I can offer is anecdotal evidence from many professional women whose kids reached age three: "All of a sudden I've got time to think again." For myself, I will say that from the time my first child was born in 1979 until the time in 1985 when my youngest approached age three, I was in survival mode, which is to say: I did my job, I took good care of people, but in retrospect it seems as though I never once brought my head up to look around.

Everything was going well with the practice during those years. It was growing beyond my expectations. I contrast those early North Creek-practice years with the way I'd felt during that summer residency at the veterans' hospital in Seattle. On the prior occasion it had been the drive to work with the white-knuckle dread that I somehow might not measure up to what would be expected that day.

Others no doubt go through similar bouts of worry as they are embarking on their careers. No matter what one's level of confidence or what has been demonstrated in the way of competence, there's the lingering thought that maybe somehow it isn't all going to come together. Now, at North Creek, I would drive up the hill out of the neighborhood in the mornings thinking: "I wonder how many other people are looking forward to their day as much as I am." It wasn't just that I was fulfilled in my work, though I was. My happiness also derived from knowing about the general advancement of women in my profession as evidenced by the number of women who were going on staff at the Everett hospitals. There had been just the three of us when I came to my practice, but just a few years later there were as many as fifty. The need for women in medicine was finally being filled. Because it was, I began to see myself less as a pioneer among women family doctors and more as a public voice for women's health issues.

That public role came to pass partly as a result of becoming medical director of the Helen Jackson Center for Women. The widow of Sen. Henry "Scoop" Jackson had become nearly as well known and valued a community resource as Scoop had been until the massive heart attack claimed the man who was one of Washington State's most renowned world citizens. Mrs. Jackson continues her activities with the Helen Jackson Foundation, which came into existence in the mid-1980s, its initial goal being to see to it that space was reserved at Everett General Hospital for women to come and have mammograms. It became an organization through which the staff members and I could bring to the fore women's issues in health-care. I got involved in giving lectures on osteoporosis, diabetes, birth control, menopause, and other subjects. Early on, it occurred to me that lecturing and raising issues in such a public forum and reaching such a relatively large number of people was extremely valuable. It was very different from what could be accomplished going one-on-one in a medical office.

In addition to addressing professional forums, the Jackson Foundation put me in the public spotlight. It gave me a firsthand feeling for the tempestuous controversy that can attend medical discussions. In retrospect I only wish the subject had been general family practice or abortion rather than what it was: breast cancer. I was called upon to appear in a forum about breast cancer. The event was staged by a Seattle television station, which also had invited a physician who was supposed to be a breast-cancer authority. The third and "star" member of the panel was a well-known actress whose experiences with breast cancer had been recounted copiously in virtually all media. Unbeknownst to anyone, another panel member arrived in the person of the actress's husband. The husband's presence immediately created problems, not the least of which was the fact that the second physician bailed out of the production at the last minute. The other doctor hadn't appreciated being baited by the husband during what was supposed to be a cordial session in the "green room" prior to the program. That left me, a physician whose specialty was not breast cancer, to in effect debate the subject with the husband of a well-known victim of the disease. I had, here again, been included on the panel strictly as a family physician. I insisted to the producers that I was not a specialist and that I would only appear to give general opinions about women's health matters.

Instead I found myself thrown rather abruptly into the hurly-burly of talk TV. The experience led me to the conclusion that I simply cannot debate certain medical ideas. I certainly would be unwilling to debate abortion matters, especially if it were with someone of such dubious authority as my unexpected copanelist. Under certain circumstances I might not have minded having to suffice as the emergency breast-cancer authority. But during every commercial break the husband would turn to me and say something like: "How do you know what you're saying is true? I happen to think you're wrong. After all, you're not a specialist, you're just a G.P." He sneered at the notion of family practice, letting it be known that he, a lay person as far as medicine was concerned, knew better than the physicians about breast-cancer treatment. It would have been better for all concerned had the husband left the medical discussion to the doctor, especially when I was offering my opinions—correct and well-informed—about lumpectomies. Then again, it would be better during any abortion debate if the hysterical and ill-informed were to leave the discussion to the women and their providers. An irony associated with the way the antichoice crowd frames the abortion debate is that the procedure is somehow dreadful. As we'll see in subsequent chapters, the procedure actually is relatively brief and painless.

My assertion about lumpectomy was as follows: A lot more women, instead of losing a breast, would do as well with lumpectomies and local radiation. This was being shown at the time to be as effective as the more radical breast-removal procedures and potentially much less traumatic. I noted that it wasn't changing women's life spans to have a lump rather than an entire breast removed. But this was at a time when it was considered extremely brash to be saying this out loud, even though I was comfortable that I had very good evidence to quote. Surgeons were saying that if it were them or their wife they'd recommend breast-removal. What I was saying was: "If I had breast cancer, then knowing what I know about it I'd opt for a lumpectomy."

One of the most horrible surgeries I'd ever attended during my training was a mastectomy. It occurred to me then and still does that "yes, it's just a piece of flesh," and "no, we shouldn't be completely enslaved by how we look," and "no, a breast isn't so sexually important that you couldn't survive without it." On the other hand, I also have strong feelings about performing surgery with respect for the appendages that are affected. I felt that surgeons had done amputations with far more respect for a lost limb than they had that time with the breast-removal. I was appalled at how the surgery was done. It was clear to me that the attitude was this: this breast is just a thing in the way. It's got cancer in it so let's just hurry up and get it out of there. I felt that the issue was much more complicated.

At the same time I do agree that the breast—both absence and presence of it—has been sexualized beyond necessity. The ideal would be if we all could accept exactly how we look. But I have advised women who feel horrible about their breasts that they have every right to change them without judgment from me or anybody else. I tell them: "Look, you seem to be really suffering about your breasts, and I can't expect you to go out and change society so that it will ignore this aspect of your appearance. So, yeah, I know this plastic surgeon who can do a good job of enlarging your breasts if that's what is going to make you feel whole and happy about yourself." I still feel fine about that because studies have been contradictory about whether or not there are any bad health effects from breast implants.

Anyway, the ultimate decision-maker in this and other matters of elective surgery should be the patient. Early on, I learned two critical health-care lessons. The first is that it's nearly impossible to force a patient to make a change in her or his life. How much futile lecturing, for example, has gone toward getting patients to accept the fact that they ought to change lifestyle decisions about, say, smoking or unsafe sex? Then I came to realize that the corollary to lesson one is: As a physician I don't have to have anything emotionally invested in whether or not patients change their lifestyles. The reason I'm here is to give a medical opinion, not to be judgmental after presenting the facts and arguing for the health path I favor. My attitude as a family physician is simple: I'm going to continue caring for you even if you don't take my advice and quit doing what I've told you is harmful.

There are, of course, the well-documented harmful lifestyle decisions mentioned above. Obviously there's nothing to recommend smoking or unsafe sexual behavior. Yet, by the mid-1980s I was realizing that people's behavioral decisions were based on many issues including unhappy childhoods. This was reinforced time and again by talking with patients. Every time I would hear of the various forms of past child abuse affecting my adult patients, I would find myself consciously seeking out similar anecdotal information from others. So it occurred to me that I should ask the questions more often. If patients, for example, came from homes in which the parents abused alcohol, then that led to a whole other set of problems. If the patients themselves abused drugs or alcohol, then that led to yet another set of problems. So in the process of taking careful medical histories I became even more politicized about the practice of medicine in terms of what could be done—and what couldn't be done—to make people healthier by the time they reach adulthood. And it occurred to me that maybe by not asking the right questions I could be ignoring huge health-care problems. So I asked more questions, learned more about my patients, and could develop better treatment plans. That's the goal of a good family physician.

But here again, "abuse" scarcely was limited to what some think of as destructive lifestyle decisions. Poverty plays an obvious role. I have a striking memory of a woman coming to me with her three children. This anecdote is among many that make me bristle when I hear some uninformed politician talk about "welfare mothers." This woman was a single mother on welfare. During the course of examining her three children I was asked by her: "Which of my kids is growing the fastest?" Their ages ranged from infant to three and five. I said: "You know, that's a very interesting question. They're all growing pretty rapidly, though at different phases of their lives. Why do you ask?" "Because," she said, "if I only have enough milk for one of them, then I want to give all of it to the one who is growing fastest and needs it most right now." My heart was so broken for that mother that I immediately redoubled my resolve to be a champion for poor women. It can be a daunting challenge, too, in a country where members of Congress try to vote themselves pay raises and keep their privileges while blithely exacerbating social inequities with flippant talk about welfare mothers driving Cadillacs. I have yet to see a welfare woman driving a Cadillac. I'm sure it's happened somewhere, sometime, but not in the experience of the poor women I have seen—and I've seen a lot of them.

So I added poverty to the list of poor-health indicators, along with ignorance about immunization, and, in some cases, an inability to even come in for treatment. There were whole cycles of dysfunctional families, starting with chronic lack of education, leading to a reduced ability to make informed choices, followed by a lack of self-esteem that predicted poor choices of partners. The latter would result in the worst possible choices about sexual activity. That, of course, would lead to unplanned pregnancies, unwanted children, and a renewal of the whole sad cycle. So many poor women lacked healthy role models for raising children. This meant that the only way a poor mother could proceed was to fall back on child-rearing the way she had been raised. Living in poverty also meant the ongoing potential for nutritional damage to the children. Politicians of the nineties talk of curbing government-sponsored nutritional programs, utterly unaware of or callous to the idea that generations of children already have grown up undernourished. Chronic lack of nutrition itself caused its share of stress within families, to say nothing of the other problems associated with poverty. All of this created stress that resulted in adults admitting to me that as children they'd heard at home that "they wished they hadn't had me, that I was a mistake."

It became, then, axiomatic that a good starting point for proper personal and familial development would at least be for people to be happy about this little human being coming into the world. If the child were wanted, it didn't necessarily guarantee healthy development. But it sure gave the child a leg up in the world by providing a basic support system. Moreover, if families could be helped with not having so many unwanted children, then their financial burden could be eased, or at least not further exacerbated.

For me, then, it became pretty clear that women caught in the poverty cycle needed lots of help in learning that they really could make decisions about the size of their families. If they could (a) become persuaded to think in terms of controlling their own reproductive lives and (b) be afforded the opportunity to get abortions, then they would be on their way toward lives far less oppressive than the ongoing poverty cycle had produced. At the same time, what with the budding Reagan-Bush years and the nurturing of the wealthy elite at the expense of the poor and powerless, the political climate was becoming increasingly hostile toward abortion. The right-wing patriarchy didn't give a damn about children once they were born into hopeless circumstances. But this same cabal of rich conservatives sure wasn't going to allow women easy access to abortion information—not if the conservative-religious voting bloc could be easily assuaged and won over by antichoice rhetoric. The Reagan administration played to its fundamentalist political support and started cutting Medicaid funding for abortions. Naturally poor women were the first ones to suffer. If you were a rich woman—and consider how many of them may have had abortions after having gotten pregnant with men who claim to be antichoice—then you obviously could afford any reproductive decision you chose. Child-rearing expenses were scarcely a problem for the wealthy, and neither was seeking a good private abortion clinic. In other words, the part of the population that would have been best served by being given access to controlling the birth of unwanted children became the segment least capable of doing so.

At the time, I figured I was doing what I could for my patients by staying a family doctor. I did what I could for the world at large by being medical director at Helen Jackson Center and speaking out, talking with the press, and addressing anyone who would listen. Then I decided to do what I thought was important for children of alcoholic parents by simultaneously being medical director of an alcohol-treatment program.

In addition to these three demanding roles, I went back to something I'd all but abandoned for five years. By 1985, with my children more independent, I was able to spend a half-day a month relieving Dr. George Denniston again, doing abortions at his Seattle clinic. When I had graduated from my residency, Dr. Denniston had wanted me to take over his clinic. I told him I wasn't ready to be strictly an abortion doctor and that I needed to be a family doctor, applying the ideas that had compelled me to be a physician in the first place.

When I went back to help him, I still wasn't interested in taking over, given my other responsibilities. Yet, in 1986 I did just that.* This allowed me to add to my work an outlet for how I felt politically about unwanted pregnancies. I was there a half-day a week at that point, which still left me with four jobs: family physician; medical director of two programs; and now owner, medical director, and abortion doctor at my own clinic. I had two kids, a husband, and a house, and, it somehow seems in retrospect, a life beyond all that. Perhaps needless to say, that kind of craziness took its toll within a couple of years.

All of this was happening at the same time that conservative politics had swept America. The fraudulent conservatism embodied by what amounted to a figurehead president meant no social program—no humanitarian assumption about families in need—was safe anymore. I became much more intense and deliberate about researching candidates and publicly supporting likeminded people. I was asked to run for office but it was clear then and remains so now that I wouldn't be as effective as a politician. Fear and misinformation—and both at once, as witnessed by radio-talk-show rhetoric—conspire to prevent positive change. Consider Bill Clinton, for example, coming into office with this supposed great desire—maybe even mandate—to change the attitudes of Americans and thus the condition of those less well off. Then, as change is advocated and implemented, the voter reaction two years later is fear and anger. These probably are just the normal human responses to proposed change. From experience with patients, I've concluded that making a change in attitude and behavior is the scariest thing imaginable to most people. Likewise, it's equally difficult trying to dissuade people from being afraid of change. It's much easier to remain afraid than to commit to making the change. Bad as the status quo may be, there's a kind of perverse security in knowing what to expect rather than accepting change.

---

*Dr. Denniston has now retired from abortion practice, but he continues to be active in national and international population through his nonprofit organization, Population Dynamics.

Toward the latter stages of my tenure at the family-practice clinic, it became apparent that a lot of patients were dependent on me. A specialist could say: "Okay, I've checked out your aching gut, we've scoped you up and down and there's nothing wrong with you." As a family physician, though, I still needed to take that person aside and say: "We've decided there's nothing serious happening to you physically right now. Then again, you've still got this stomach problem." That's when the hard work began, and I must have given my "stress-box" lecture ten times a day for the final five years of my practice.

The lecture in essence is: We're all born with an ability to tolerate stress. We're also all probably born with the same size box to hold the stress. Some of us pour stuff into the box at faster rates than others. When your stress box is full you either have to stop the stresses coming in, which none of us has ever figured out how to do, or increase the drainage rate. If you don't, what will happen is exactly what's happening to you: You'll get an excess of adrenaline, which we used to use during cave-dwelling days to stand in front of a sabertooth tiger and either kill it or run away. Nowadays we're faced with being unable to either run away or relieve our aggression in any significant way, but the adrenaline still comes. And it will affect any physical system that happens to be the weakest. For some it will be headaches and for others it'll be hypertension or stomach aches. In extreme cases, it results in what is misidentified as "unprovoked" violence.

Counseling patients in stress tolerance is itself a task that takes a huge amount of tolerance, patience, and the ability to divest yourself as a physician of the problems being described. I came to realize that I could point out all sorts of useful information to people and I still wouldn't be able to fix their lives or their health problems, or sometimes, for that matter, even say anything to give them some satisfaction. It's just hard talking to people's pain, especially given the patent futility I've described. Nevertheless I would tell patients that they needn't be sick to see me. They could come in once a week and we'd spend fifteen minutes together, it would be their time and we'd talk about whatever they wanted. In effect, then, I suddenly found myself doing family medicine/psychotherapy. I wasn't sure where I was taking them, but I knew if I didn't give them the fifteen minutes a week they'd call me after hours or have some other crisis. Some patients reached a point where they only needed to come in once a month or maybe every three months. But they'd always be there with their problems that were always going to be the same, and I knew that I was going to have to put a lot of energy into seeing if we couldn't gain insight. Most of these patients were women. I saw one woman, for example, for seven years before she finally agreed to try psychotherapy.

What caused the stress? The same change-related issues we talk about now. Roles for men and women were no longer as clearly defined as they had been during, say, the fifties. It was becoming apparent that a woman's role was to make money outside the home and contribute to a two-income lifestyle that grew harder to sustain with every new financial demand (providing for additional children, medical expenses, college tuition, etc.). But at the same time women's other roles weren't changing, domestic responsibilities in particular. The plight of the single mother immediately comes to mind. Other women experienced a shift in relationships from which developed serious negative consequences when, say, she would gain confidence and announce that she was going to go back to school and try to improve herself or reach a long sought-after goal. Some couples had difficulty handing the strain of these life choices. Add physical illnesses on top of these family stresses and the cumulative effect was often enormous. People suddenly didn't feel confident about how they were bringing up their kids. This self-consciousness and frustration came about at a time when there were fewer and fewer social-support systems, a progressively more violent society and popular culture, while drug use and gun possession were spiraling out of control. Neighborhoods were rapidly becoming unsafe if not openly hostile. Even in areas with relatively low crime, neighbors spent much less time with one another and often were total strangers.

People had become extremely afraid of what they had formerly viewed in isolation and at a significant distance.

Despite the career demands, I felt committed to the idea that I could not or would not say to anyone: "Sorry, but I just can't help you anymore." In retrospect, I probably could have. But in listening to them I'd think, "Yeah, you're absolutely right. The world is really giving you a raw deal, and I just can't bring myself to be one more person giving you a hard time." It felt very good to say to patients: "Just take a nice walk for twenty minutes three times a week, and you'll feel much better." Of course that often was greeted with: "C'mon, doc, just gimme a pill!" And then I'd repeat the mantra about the walk and the stress box, all the while I'd be thinking: "This is what it's getting down to? This is what I have to offer to people? Go for a walk three times a week?"

It dawned on me how very much I needed to move in a direction that would bring focus to my professional life. I need to be effective to make a real difference in people's lives. I wasn't sure if my place was in alcohol treatment because I couldn't honestly say I was happy with the results of my work there. The Helen Jackson Center was moving toward an approach demanding more in-hospital attention rather than the less lucrative out-of-hospital services. To be honest, I was feeling the pressures of having four jobs. My family-practice senior partner had served notice that he'd be moving on, leaving me to wonder whether that meant I'd be delivering everybody's babies at all hours of the night. Then again, could I still call myself a family physician if I wasn't doing deliveries anymore? Possibly, but I'd no longer be able to make enough money to stay in business. I even started working more at the abortion clinic to make enough of an increased salary there that I could continue my work at my North Creek clinic even though the latter was not financially stable.

After a couple of years of this intense workload, I finally had to conclude that it was okay to focus my efforts strictly on the abortion clinic. By specializing, I could be a lot more effective than I had been while trying to spread myself over both facilities. I had no illusion that I would necessarily change anybody's lifestyle in any significant way—I might not even change their attitudes—but I might be meeting them at a point in their lives when they could hear something that would make them feel more optimistic about themselves. I could meet them at a time when they'd be treated with respect, consideration, and empathy. This, if nothing else, was a valuable thing to do, especially at a time when women's roles were changing and stress levels were intensifying. Moreover, for each client who wishes to see me, I would be in a position to prevent an unwanted birth. That thought alone gave me a feeling of self-worth and professional fulfillment because of what I'd seen of unwanted children in the past.

Recalling that sequence of events I am more sure than ever that my final career choice made eminent good sense. Having said this, those were very trying times for me. I was in therapy myself then, and it was tremendously useful. It gave me an outlet for asking: "What can I let go of?" For a time it seemed as though I was going to keep adding jobs and responsibilities with the unrealistic goal of meeting everybody's needs. Not surprisingly, I was drained and had to realize that I was not giving anybody what they needed.

After much thought and discussion with John, I acquired the abortion clinic in January 1986. We sold our family practice in October 1988, after which I worked a couple of days each week at another family practice, phasing out my patients and rationalizing that they also needed time to let go of me. Then my family and I took six months off, which was the perfect transition for several reasons. One, it's a practical way to end a family practice, because you literally disappear for half a year. Moreover, it was one of the best things John and I had ever done, since it gave us much needed time with our kids. We really jelled as a family. For John and me it brought back wonderful memories of the late 1970s when we traveled to exotic areas of the world. Then there'd been the time spent starting our respective medical practices and having a family. We'd always been clear on having two children, so that wasn't an issue. Then, with the youngest turning three, there was the constant realization of how rushed we were. When would there ever come a time to be together?

So we escaped more or less and lived in southern France in a village near Avignon. It was as idyllic as one could imagine. The boys were enrolled in school there and John and I became familiar with the lives of the locals. Our departure for this Mediterranean getaway was hastened by the tragic accidental death of the family of one of the physicians we knew in Everett. A car of a drunk driver jumped a median and hit them head on killing the entire family. That reminder of your own mortality strengthened our resolve to do what we felt was important for ourselves and our children.

The adventure in France was utterly serendipitous for a number of reasons, not the least of which was that it was a quiet, civilized prelude to the hard work waiting back home. Upon our return, I came to understand that perhaps the hardest part of being an abortion provider is trying to dissuade public opinion about what doesn't happen at my clinic and what does.

9

The Reality of the Clinic

The terminology used in the abortion debate has been one-sided for so long that it's no wonder the public has little if any idea what actually happens when a woman comes to a clinic such as mine. In the first place, we afford complete confidentiality to the women who come to us. Ironically, that may be detrimental to the cause of bringing society at large to a better understanding about abortion. Ideally there should be an army of women comfortable with the decision they made and ready to explain the experience of abortion to anybody who will listen. Unfortunately, society has imposed shame upon the procedure so that women have become reticent. My hope is that this won't always be the case. This chapter will describe in detail and as accurately as I can what actually goes on at a well-run abortion clinic.

When trying to picture something about which we have little knowledge but harbor many assumptions, the mind races with wild imaginings. I think the average person imagines a clinic as a place that is shabby looking or at least sterile looking and uninviting.

Some may assume that the personnel aren't professional. Maybe it's not quite clear in the mind's eye that everything is clean. The more radical antichoice assessment would be that there's a lot of blood everywhere, a lot of screaming going on, and plenty of loud noise and machinery. Some have insisted that we use scissors and scalpels. At any rate this is my impression of what many people either believe to be the atmosphere or have been led to believe about it by those with a vested interest in instilling fear and mistrust. Demonizing the opposition is something countries do to one another in times of war, so it isn't surprising that those in the antichoice camp fighting what Pat Buchanan calls America's "moral war" would do the same.

When patients visit us it isn't uncommon for them to say: "Your clinic is beautiful," as though it's a big surprise. What, no screaming? No blood all over the floors? Visit a plastic surgeon's office and you expect it to be comfortable and well appointed. But an abortion clinic? Some women have been surprised by my credentials: "You went to Harvard?" I suppose they think that abortion doctors can't or don't earn degrees from prestigious schools or do their residencies at distinguished hospitals. I tell them: "Yes, I chose to do this work. This is an honorable profession."

Solving (or at least mitigating) our identity problem could be accomplished, I suppose, by running tours through the clinic while women are having abortions. That way everyone who cares so much about reproductive rights could see precisely what goes on. Of course, such a wholesale violation of patient privacy wouldn't do, but it might help dissuade those who chant the usual American antichoice abortion glossary: "murder," "killer," "blood on the walls," and so forth.

The reality is that our clinic is a relatively placid place. Some women add to this sense when they come in and stage what amounts to rituals around the procedures. A patient came in recently with her partner and brought candles, clearly making the experience a ritual way of saying: "I'm proud of myself for making this choice, but I'm also sad about the choice. I'll grieve the loss and then move on in my life." These demonstrations are infrequent, mainly because women carry shame, guilt, and sadness as their major abortion-related emotions. Would they feel these emotions if certain elements of society didn't insist that abortion is dishonorable? I don't think so.

The shame derives directly from society's view that abortion is something bad. The prevailing thought on the subject seems to be: We're not sure we like it at all for ourselves; we think maybe it's all right or at least understandable in the case of a woman who has been raped or has been a victim of incest; we're a little worried that women are just doing this for convenience sake. No woman makes this decision lightly or in a moral vacuum—she thinks and feels long and hard about it.

When the antichoice people use terms such as "murder" and "kill" and "blood-dripping abortionists," they employ these highly charged words to create an aura intended to dissuade women who face the abortion decision. We who are prochoice always talk about changing the language of abortion. But we're not going to change the language until we all agree that abortion is a valid, moral, and honorable decision. It's one thing to say: "Well, there are too many abortions, I wish we didn't have to do them anymore and hope that the day would come when we'd put ourselves out of business." But that dismisses the reality of women's ongoing need to not be pregnant under certain circumstances. Society has no apparent strong objections to the circumstances under which a women gets pregnant. Men are able to impregnate women without suffering any consequences. Society doesn't say to men: "Look, you're at least partly responsible for this embryo having been fertilized, and consequently we're going to hold you responsible for cosupport if a baby is born." Society is only too willing, however, to insist on an opinion in the case of the woman who is dealing with an unwanted pregnancy. The antichoice view is: "Hey, you got pregnant, and now we insist that you deliver a baby—with or without the father's help, or anyone else's for that matter."

Denying the reality of reproductive freedom for women also fails to honor women. Antichoice rhetoric always falls back on the notion that women who make choices about their own reproductive lives are somehow dishonorable. When women ask me how I can perform abortions every day, I tell them that I don't consider the work to be a chore or an imposition. On the contrary, I'm honored to be part of their decision-making process. It seems obvious that many women aren't able to imagine how rewarding it is for me to watch a female patient take steps on her path through life—steps that will empower her and make her able to be responsible for herself and her family.

My ideal world would have women emerge from an abortion clinic proud in the knowledge that they have made a very difficult choice, worked through the consequences, dealt as best they can with grief issues, and are ready to move on with their lives. The rest of us should stand by them, respecting their decision. I don't see this being the case anytime soon, particularly not in view of what happened during the 1994 midterm elections and the prospect of amplified antichoice rhetoric raising its ugly head in the '96 campaigns. But if society would just dare to frame the abortion conversation in terms of the *woman's* life, then it would have come a long way. The abortion controversy, after all, is much less about children than about control over what women may do with their own lives. It's terribly frightening for many in a patriarchal society—one that didn't even let women vote until 1920—to think that women could control when and if they have children. The general acceptance of that control may not even come in my lifetime, just as voting rights didn't arrive in time for women who wrote about society's "total oppression of women" as long ago as the Republican convention of 1848. But it must come some day if this country is ever to move beyond the abortion argument to more pressing issues.

A sense of shame encumbers the vast majority of the women I see at the clinic. At its worst, the shame is manifested in remarks such as: "I can't believe this is actually happening to me"; "I was always very much against abortion"; "I can't possibly tell anyone in my family"; "I have no one close to me to talk to who wouldn't feel horribly disappointed in me." That they still make the decision to have the abortion demonstrates incredible strength amid the anguish and despair felt by women facing a forced pregnancy. Even a number of women who hold many of the abortion clinic misconceptions we've outlined will still come to a clinic to end an unwanted pregnancy. They will decide to have a surgical procedure, even while harboring this antichoice belief about how horrible the experience will be.

Then there's the pervasive sense among clients that they'll have no support for their decision: "I'm all by myself and I have to do this." Yet they still show up at the clinic. They've pulled themselves together, scraped up the money, and found their way to the clinic.

There's always the prospect that they'll have to run the gauntlet of scare tactics set forth by abortion opponents: that an abortion might prevent you from ever getting pregnant again, that it might lead to breast cancer, and so forth. None of these horror stories has ever been given any medical credence, but the antichoice side keeps using them. Though the social and psychological obstacles are formidable, women here and all over the world still choose to take the risk, believing all the while that they might even die—such is the degree of hysteria that attends some antichoice propaganda. The determination and strength of these women's character never ceases to amaze me. Women come despite worries that they will run a literal gauntlet as well, through jeering antichoice protesters. I've heard many of them say how relieved they were not to see protesters around the clinic. If I held the same images of abortion that many of them do, I'm not sure I would have the courage to make the same decision.

I estimate that as many as 80 percent of those who contact us have a false—and often negative—image of what to expect. Many who have more realistic expectations are referred by friends or other physicians. Upon arriving, some say: "Oh, you've got this great art on your walls and your waiting room is so pretty." They're genuinely surprised. And no wonder, when the opposition has gotten away with establishing the terms of the debate. Besides, when would the reality of an abortion clinic ever have been discussed by most women? If it's a topic about which you've been made to feel ashamed, you're not likely to bring it up at a dinner party. Consequently, a lot of women and virtually all men are utterly unaware of the fact that many of their close friends and acquaintances have had abortions—and more than a few no doubt have had more than one.

The sense of shame is rendered so personal by society that most women bear it alone. I think they instinctively sense that any emotional burden—legitimate or otherwise—ought to be shared with their sex partners. But a profound sense of futility overshadows any sharing that might have taken place. Not that we don't see some really wonderful partnerships come in to terminate a pregnancy. Some couples come in and exhibit tremendous support for one another. In many such cases it isn't so much shame that they feel but the pure sorrow of having to give up a potential pregnancy. For most women, though, the conclusion is: "Well, it's my own damned fault." To this I respond: "Excuse me, but did you just scrape up some sperm somewhere and insert it yourself? I don't think so." I tell my own sons: "Listen, you're responsible for that sperm as soon as it leaves your body. You'd better be sure it's going some place it belongs. If it doesn't belong, then *you're* responsible for what happens." But how many other boys hear from their parents while growing up that they need to feel a similar sense of responsibility? Some boys get a vague message about "responsible sex" and some even have parents who take the trouble to insist that they use contraceptives. Contrast this with what many girls hear: "You can get pregnant—and it'll be *your* fault and *you* will have to deal with it." It's been clear as long as societies have existed that the responsibility for child-having and child-bearing rests with the woman. The responsibility of being a boy is to become educated and pursue a career. I saw a survey recently indicating that 60 percent of teenage boys want a partner who won't work outside the home, while only 20 or 30 percent of young women would prefer such an arrangement. Maybe there's a major domestic clash about to occur, because it appears that at least a third of the teenage population has unrealistic expectations.

Can we at the clinic ease the sense of shame felt by many of our patients? We can try. We tell them that we honor them for making their decision and that we regard it as a moral, responsible decision made in the best interests the patient perceives for herself and her family. Often I'll add that it's too bad making a good decision isn't always easy, and that even the fact that it may not seem right at the time doesn't invalidate the decision over the longer haul. Does this informal counseling help? It's hard to say. I play a professional role in between 2,000 and 3,000 lives a year, and if I can make even a minor contribution toward helping these women feel better about themselves and their rights, then that's good.

But shame is tough for some women to shake. Some will say: "You know, I've always viewed myself as a responsible person: well educated and I've got this good job. Yet look at me. I couldn't even keep myself from becoming pregnant." These women share a superhuman expectation about themselves. It tells them that they should never fail in contraceptive decisions or choices about having sex. When failure arises in the form of an unwanted pregnancy, it's not surprising that they feel less superhuman than before. Conversely, I witness very few instances of patients who view themselves as victims. Occasionally, a client will insist: "It's my boyfriend's fault, my father's fault, that man took advantage of me." Instead, the feeling usually is one of having failed to avoid making a bad judgment. Seldom is it acknowledged that a man failed to be responsible about when and how to have sex. It's sad to conclude, then, that after so much progress in the awareness of women's issues, many women either say they believe or actually do feel that, yes, it's always ultimately the woman's fault.

Sorrow, quite apart from the sense of shame, is exhibited in some way by virtually every woman for whom I've performed an abortion, and that's 20,000 as of 1995. The sorrow is revealed by the fact that most women cry at some point during the experience. A lot of them do so during the initial counseling, but for others it wells up just from the empathy they receive from us, like when we say: "This must really be a hard day for you." Some cry when I say during the procedure that "your uterus is rapidly emptying and it's going back to the way it was before you became pregnant." At that point they know it's really over. Sometimes they'll cry out during the procedure, but not because of pain. I'll routinely ask if they're uncomfortable and they'll invariably say, "not physically." Of course a variety of other ways exist to express sorrow—anger being a common one. But the purest visceral response is tears. Some hold off through the interviewing, through meeting with me, and even through the procedure. For them it isn't until a staff person comes in afterward and asks them how they're doing that they feel it's okay to cry. Women seem to vary as far as the people with whom they feel safe to express their sorrow. For some it's with their partner, though this is difficult to quantify because only about 30 percent of women I see are accompanied by a partner during their visit, and for many it's the person who has accompanied them to the to the clinic and been their support person in the surgery room.

The grieving process may last from several days to several years, depending on the other reactions a patient has to the process. Grief is sometimes delayed, especially if there's a lot of shame; the grief may lie sublimated and dormant for years. If women were honored for their decision as much by society as we do at the clinic, the sense of shame wouldn't even be an issue. If the abortion debate could be stated plainly in terms of women having to make their own decisions about eventualities affecting their own bodies and their own futures, then I believe the element of shame would largely disappear. Then again, of late, certain factions of the antichoice crowd have tried to exploit the notion of a woman's real or perceived longterm response to an abortion. The idea of framing the emotional response in terms of post-traumatic-stress syndrome hasn't met with any legal victory, but it exists as a threat in the form of nuisance-suit litigation. The antichoice side seems willing to consider any angle, however tenuous it may be, rather than grant the idea that a sovereign human being ought not to be dictated to by society on matters affecting the body. Granting women their rights is far too threatening.

We hear from many women that the grieving process actually ends by the time they leave the office. This is because the vast majority of women feel relieved at the end of the procedure. They can go on with their lives, which is precisely why they come to us. No matter how women choose to work through emotions accompanying their decision to abort, the fact remains that they seek us of their own volition. Those who don't come in to abortion clinics obviously have made the choice my husband and I made when we decided to have our children. Whatever their reason for either decision, their choice requires no explanation, much less an apology.

Typically the pregnant woman contacts us by phone. She may have heard about the clinic from friends or a physician, or she may even have picked us out of the phone book. I can't stress enough that to do this—to make what on the surface appears to be a random choice—attests to the strength of these women. Of those who come to us via the phone book, we find that most have made more than one call and have been attracted to us because of what they heard from the people with whom they spoke. Those contact voices may have belonged to just about anybody because my clinic is set up so that every staff member rotates between assignments: front-desk receptionists, informed-consent educators, assistants during procedures, and lab and clean-up workers. That way everyone who talks with patients on the phone knows our whole procedure and can answer virtually every question. They're able to speak to women with tremendous depth of knowledge and understanding. If I were looking for a place to have an abortion performed, that knowledge would certainly attract me. That's precisely why we're set up to provide such a high comfort level. The clinic staff member asks the patient how long she's been pregnant, about the time of her last menstrual period, and whether she needs to know more about the procedure. She's given a brief explanation of our procedure, told about costs, and informed about the counseling she'll receive when she comes in. The initial phone call might take five to fifteen minutes. As far as cost is concerned, we have a sliding fee scale. Only women who make $30,000 a year or more pay the full price of $330 (or $390 with ultrasound): most patients pay less than the full amount. Obviously we can't provide the service free of charge, although, in a more enlightened society, government health-care funding would help women to a greater degree rather than punishing them for being poor.

When callers have had all their questions answered, they make an appointment. We encourage them to bring along a support person. Patients show up at our office, fill out some demographic forms and a questionnaire about their emotional and practical feelings pertaining to the abortion: "How do you feel about the safety of abortion?" "How much support do you feel you'll get?" "How do you think you'll feel during the abortion? After the abortion?" The questionnaire helps the person serving as counselor that day get a quick look at the main sources of a patient's concern. Then the woman receives detailed information about the entire abortion procedure. She's shown models of the uterus if she's interested; she's shown the instruments that will be used; there's a book that shows pictures of the various stages of pregnancy. Women are also advised that they can feel free to see the contents of the uterus after the procedure.

All of this preliminary counseling provides time for the woman to reflect on her decision. At anytime during counseling, she can say: "You know, now that I'm here and I see firsthand what this is really going to involve, I've decided that I don't want to do this." Obviously this decision is just fine. We're not advocating abortion. We are merely insisting on the freedom to choose abortion.

Do very many women opt out of the procedure at this point? Maybe one or two out of the 250 we see each month. Less frequently —perhaps once in 500 cases—has a woman thought otherwise about having the abortion after she's met me and the procedure is about to commence. When a woman is still ambivalent at this point, I tell her to consider the following: "If you feel as though your head is saying this is the right thing to do, but your gut is telling you it agrees but is really sad about it, then you'll probably do fine. If, on the other hand, both your head and your gut are screaming at you that it isn't right, then you're probably not going to do well and I don't think you should have this abortion today." After this she may yet choose to come back another day for the procedure. Or maybe she'll choose not to. Rarer still—maybe once in a thousand procedures—a woman will have actually taken a sedative and had her defense mechanisms lowered, and still want to stop. That's fine, too. But there's a physical point beyond which I no longer can stop the procedure and I let them know about it before we get to that stage.

"Once I begin to dilate the cervix," I remind them, "we're at the point of no return."

I've never had a woman want to turn back as we approached the point of no return.

10

Having the Abortion

Some women find it necessary to apologize to us during the abortion process. We tell them they're perfectly welcome to apologize if they feel they need to, but they don't have to do it on our account. Providing this vital service is what we're here for. Some clients feel trapped by an unwanted baby and maybe they feel equally trapped about having an abortion. Either way, we're available to help them out of their trap. We try very hard not to be judgmental. Perhaps what they're actually doing is reacting to the shame we discussed in the previous chapter. Those of us at the clinic represent the nearest approximation to society at large, and what the women actually are doing is trying to apologize to the world for the decision they've made. In truth, it's the world that should be apologizing to them for imposing such needless feelings of shame.

The abortion itself can take as little as a few minutes to perform, though we tell women to reserve three hours of maximum office time. But if they're the first patient of the day, less than nine weeks pregnant, and very clear about their decision, then a woman with an

8:45 A.M. appointment could figure on being out of the office by 9:30. But the vagaries of patient flow and paper work are such that it may take longer. The actual time lying down with a speculum in the vagina may vary from seven minutes for women in the early stages of pregnancy to thirty minutes for those progressed to sixteen weeks or more.

I have a running commentary that I do with patients, so that they know during the entire process what's going to happen: This will be the speculum . . . this is iodine soap. . . . Now you may get a little come-and-go cramping over the next minute as I do the anesthetic injection. . . . Now you may get a little rapid heart rate. . . . I'm going to open your cervix now. I only need to dilate to seven or eight millimeters from five millimeters for a woman who is seven or eight weeks pregnant or less. By the time I finish telling her what to expect from the dilation, I'm already done with this part of the procedure—and sometimes done with the entire procedure. I'll tell her to expect to feel some pulling and tugging, but that it won't really hurt. As I see and feel the emptying of the uterus I'll warn her that this is when the cramping will start. Sometimes the procedure goes so fast I have to interrupt the running commentary to tell the woman we're done.

When you've performed as many abortion procedures as I have there's not any fumbling around with getting things ready. When I teach residents, all procedures take nominally longer than they would if I weren't teaching. But it's not as though a normal ten-minute procedure would take a half hour. It's more a matter of a couple of extra minutes to allow for precise explanation every step of the way. When I'm teaching I obviously want to make certain that observers know precisely what I'm doing at every juncture and why I'm doing it. Women are told at the time they make their appointments that there will be two doctors during their procedures. They are told this again at their counseling session and can of course refuse to have more than myself in the room although women rarely do refuse, especially with female residents.

As for the level of discomfort during the procedure, I can't speak for each patient, though I can report what appears to be the case. My own abortion was done without anesthetic and at a later stage than virtually all the procedures I've performed, so I can't empathize precisely with the women I've treated. Some women speak to us in normal voices throughout the entire procedure. Some say: "Ouch, that hurts," or they take a quick in-drawn breath. With some we work on Lamaze-style breathing to help them through the final few minutes of cramping. Then there are women who cry out, and for them there's really nothing we can do short of general anesthesia to make them feel better. So it's hard to tell patients what to expect in the way of pain. I do tell them that it's nothing unbearable and nothing they'll remember as the most horrible thing that ever happened to them. Women who have given birth say that abortion is nothing compared with labor. At least 80 and perhaps 90 percent say the pain isn't as bad as they expected it to be. As for long-term discomfort, most women say they haven't had any cramping after leaving the office. Some call back to report "something going on." Maybe there's a little clot stuck or they have blood in their uterus or they have an infection. Those are the ones who are cramping afterward, but the others won't report anything more than a little soreness. As for complications beyond soreness and minor cramping, my rate is 0.1 percent, or one in a thousand.

We tell women to refrain from sex for two weeks after the abortion. As part of the procedure, we opened the cervix—the mouth of the uterus—and this encourages more germs to enter. While performing the abortion, then, we've essentially bared the surface of the uterus. After the procedure there's also a much lighter healing coat on the uterine lining, making the area much more susceptible to infection. Thirty percent of the women follow through with our checkup procedure by coming back in two weeks. That figure jibes with the national average. The follow-up, which is part of the cost of the whole procedure, simply allows women the opportunity to avail themselves of checkup care. Of the remaining 70 percent, I estimate at least a third go to subsequent checkups with their own private physicians. The rest—maybe 50 percent of all women who have abortions—decide not to return for follow-up after the procedure. Getting on with their lives, of course, was what prompted them to seek the treatment in the first place. The goal was to go back to the condition of not being pregnant.

Of those who return to see us, the demeanor is quite cheerful after two weeks. Normally what we hear is: "Tell Dr. Poppema I'm fine." Here again, this is a selective group composed of women who willingly return for the checkup, so maybe it doesn't do to draw any scientific conclusions about post-abortion attitude based on the followup visits. Obviously my staff and I welcome all comments and just as obviously we're gratified to hear that patients not only have responded well after the procedure but also have been happy to make our acquaintance.

Our records indicate repeat visits of women who come to us seeking subsequent abortions. It isn't unusual for women to come in for a second or third abortion. Even a sixth abortion, while unusual, isn't unheard of. Some women, I believe, don't come back to the same clinic for subsequent abortions because they're so ashamed of having an unwanted pregnancy again and they're worried that we'll be judgmental. I can't speak for other clinics, but I can assure them that we won't be at my clinic. I'm aware that even among the prochoice community it's not unusual for clinic personnel to be judgmental: "Well, I can see needing one abortion, but what's going on if they're having two and three? And how could she have not learned her lesson after six abortions?" Patients sometimes come in echoing such a judgment. In response we can only say: "Look, clearly you didn't do this on purpose. Obviously no one would go out of her way to get pregnant just so that she could come to this clinic for abortions. No one considers abortion an enviable goal in and of itself. It's a choice that must be confronted only after sustaining an unwanted pregnancy. Clearly you were doing the best you could with birth control. And until we have a 100-percent-effective birth-control method that's not user-dependent and has no side effects, situations like this are going to happen."

There are psychological factors that come into play regarding re- *
peated unwanted pregnancies. Maybe some women process a traumatic event improperly and unwittingly keep falling into the same behavioral situation. Possibly the birth-control failure has to do with the fact that there's been a very unequal power relationship between the woman and her sexual partner. But in individual cases where women come to us with repeated need for abortion, I don't speculate as to why. I tell them: "I know you don't do this on purpose so that you can have abortions. You're here again, so you're obviously having a hard time with birth control." My whole point is: "What a drag for you that this happened, and I'm glad we're here to help you." Women will say: "Oh, I'll never do this again. I'll never get pregnant again." And I say: "I'm sure you're going to try, and it's a good approach. But if anything untoward occurs we'll be here to help you." I feel a strong need to add that affirmation, because these women are already setting themselves up to feel horrible if they have another failure in their lives. Many of them have experienced far too much failure as it is, even if a lot of it was caused by circumstances over which they had little if any control.

I've mentioned that many sex partners do accompany women to the clinic. In my experience, though, only twice has a man come storming in protesting the procedure. That's twice out of thousands of abortions. As it happened I wasn't on the premises on one occasion, but the staff said he came in shouting: "You're killing my baby." He left without the need for police intervention. On another occasion a man came in and dragged his partner out of the clinic, telling her: "You can't have this done, this is my baby." So these instances are comparatively rare for us, and I don't really know why that is. It could have to do with many men not even knowing their partner is pregnant and getting an abortion. Fortunately women aren't required to get the consent of sexual partners, who, to my way of thinking, tacitly granted the consent by participating in sex to begin with.

As for external obstruction, we experienced most of ours during the late eighties and early nineties. During the most recent two years we've only seen our one regular stalker once in the parking lot since we got an injunction against him. That one time he was only in his car rather than out doing his usual routine: walking around cars and reciting the rosary. This no doubt has given pause to all kinds of people who come to the neighboring medical offices in our building for dental and other medical care. Our usual protester, at any rate, is a member of the local antichoice community. Prior to his initial arrival, during the early days of Operation Rescue in 1988 and 1989, we spent many a day in court seeking injunctions against any protesters coming onto our premises. Part of the reason for our relatively limited experience with protest and physical obstruction has to do precisely with the way we chose our location. Our clinic is in a medical center beyond a huge parking lot, which is off of a side street. The medical complex includes a number of other offices staffed by people with a variety of political persuasions. Because it's virtually impossible to identify the nature of our patients' medical needs as they move through the parking lot and into the complex, sidewalk preaching has been limited lately, though protesters had been hanging around with their ugly signs for a number of years. As it happens, there are some health-care providers in the complex who are also fundamentalist-Christians and we get along with them in a benign coexistence. Sometimes, when our patients would mistakenly walk into the fundamentalists' office and ask directions to the abortion clinic, our neighbors would refuse to help them with directions. But that's about as far as any problems have gone, possibly because we've been a highly professional clinic that hasn't brought on any great public spectacle.

Privately we've had a few uncomfortable moments. A few slogan-chanting antichoice zealots have invaded the clinic. A prominent antichoice man sat in our office unbeknownst to any of us for three hours one day. It was a busy day and nobody knew whether he was somebody's father or partner or chauffeur or what. Then one of the patients finally pointed out to us that the guy was passing out antiabortion literature. One of the staff called him to the front desk to ask him what he wanted and he demanded to "talk to Dr. Poppema about having her stop murdering babies." After our initial shock wore off, he was asked to leave and hasn't been back.

The police in our jurisdiction have been incredibly responsive whenever we've needed to call them. They've even dispatched female officers, which provides special support for us—not that the male police haven't been supportive. They've been willing to show up in court for us, too, which is a step beyond what some officers have been willing to take. In this same region, for example, we have the 1994 case of a state patrolman being charged with having stopped a young couple on their way to an abortion clinic and lecturing them about the woman's decision. The couple was detained without just cause and subsequently filed charges against the officer, who has become something of a martyr in antichoice circles. Yet, even some who are against women's reproductive rights were appalled that an on-duty state-police officer charged with doing the public's business would detain a young couple after learning they were on their way to an abortion clinic. It should have occurred to him that his oath of conduct ended in such instances with citing the driver for speeding.

Such self-styled "interventions" clearly haven't affected the number of women seeking our services. Our clinic is one of few in the country that has seen a slight but definite increase in patient load during the past eight years. Abortion numbers are down nationally, and the Washington State Department of Social and Health Services tells us that demand for the procedure is down in the state as much as 10 percent during the past five years. Nationally abortion is said to be down about 2 percent during the same period. Whether this represents a trend is difficult to tell, since during the two decades of legalized abortion there have been variations of as much as plus or minus 10 percent per year. Diminishing demand is one reason prompting some abortion clinics to close. Other reasons include the fact that the procedure brings in minimal revenue compared with other types of health-care treatments, especially considering the costs associated with rebuilding and repairing their facilities after damage caused at the hands of antichoice extremists. High costs also stem from insurance premiums, to say nothing of the need to pay decent wages and benefits to highly qualified staff members. Given all that it costs to run a good clinic, it's a wonder more aren't closing. It speaks to the dedication of such staffs that the prevailing adversities don't even slow them down except for the temporary shut-downs in extreme cases. But even the heroic operators of the Massachusetts clinic at which women were killed in December 1994 were able to reopen after a short time. And, sure enough, anti-choice people who had either refused to denounce the attack or had done so indifferently or inadequately were back protesting within days of the violence.

I keep ten employees on staff, with all but one or two on the premises during the hours we're open. Our clinic is busy largely because of its reputation, and partly because the location tends to draw a lot of women from a large and specific geographic location. Our patients primarily are low-income women to the extent that only about three out of 200 pay the full fee. We see primarily white patients, which has a lot to do with the demographic make-up of the area we serve. The demographics even are reflected in our present staff, which includes two Asian-American woman and the rest white. Our salary structure includes five years' worth of step increases, though many staff members will have left within five years. We've not yet had any employees go from our clinic to another abortion facility. Several have gone on to medical school, several more to nursing school, and one to the Harvard School of Public Health. Another received a full scholarship to the domestic-violence program at Duke University. Most leave because they've reached a juncture in their lives and need to continue their education or find their special place in the women's health-care system. All women we hire either are college graduates or have worked so long in the field that they have commensurate education. The women we hire are chosen much more for their commitment to feminist ideals and reproductive clinics than their past training. For those who haven't worked in the field and don't have a lot of medical background, we have a very specific training program. That often makes the more recently hired staff women less equal as a practical matter than those who have been around longer. With the exception of me, the executive director, and another provider, all staff members are equal and each is capable of virtually every non-abortion-providing duty at the clinic. This is completely different from, say, the Planned Parenthood system, in which an employee is *specifically* a receptionist or a counselor or a lab person. I'm not criticizing the work Planned Parenthood does. But operating as we do, with such versatility, helps us keep our staff small and efficient, and if only for those reasons it represents a better model for an abortion clinic. There's very little bureaucracy with us, which also, incidentally, is unlike the way most general medical clinics are run.

Typically it takes three months to train one of my staff members. The training involves studying manuals, attending lectures, and, of course, observing. During the first four weeks of the training period the staff woman has no independent contact with the patients. By the time the trainee has learned every phase of the process, my staff is not only better prepared to deal with all the patients' needs, but probably more motivated than if each member were coming in and doing the same task every day.

I don't get staff women who say: "Aw, let's schedule lightly today, because all of us are tired." or: "I don't feel like working so I'm not going to go in today." That sort of attitude wouldn't work with the level of intensity that prevails every day at our clinic. Certainly it wouldn't have helped much in the case of the woman who came to see us last year for an infection check—just a few hours before giving birth to a full-term baby. Denial, as I'm only too aware from my own experience, is a powerful human response to adverse situations. It obviously applied in this instance. We'd seen this woman for a pregnancy termination three years before. This time she called the office complaining of some vaginal discharge and abdominal pain, and that she felt horrible. We determined that this wasn't an emergency consequence from a recent surgical procedure. But we had her come in right away on the assumption that it could have been something gastrointestinal or vaginitis or ovarian cysts. When she came in one of the staff women performed a pelvic exam, took a sample of cervical mucus and put it under the microscope prior to what was to be my examination of the woman. The next thing I knew I was wanted in the examination room "right away." Something very important was going on—something that had nothing to do with any of the abortion patients who were there that day. When I entered the room the staff woman told me there was "something weird" in the woman's vagina and that she couldn't find the cervix. This poor woman was writhing on the examination table with fluid here and there, dripping all over the place. The diagnosis was obvious.

After examining her I realized that, not only was she in labor, but she had just a rim of cervix left and the baby's head was in what we call a Plus Two position: the birth could occur at any time. When the woman said, "I can't possibly be pregnant," I had to reply, "You may well believe that but your abdomen is indicating otherwise." She insisted: "But I can't have a baby. I won't have a baby." "Well," I said, "I'm sorry but that's no longer an option. You will be having a baby soon. Whether you keep it or not is a decision you'll have to make, but there are no options on having the baby."

Since I'd been the only medical contact she'd had in the past four years, she wanted me to come to the hospital with her. I couldn't go because I had commitments to other surgical patients. I felt perfectly comfortable delivering the baby right then and there, but our clinic—for obvious reasons—doesn't really have any infant-resuscitation equipment. Besides, I had no information about the pregnancy. So we called a medical-emergency unit as a backup in case we actually did wind up delivering. It had also occurred to me that we still had a whole roomful of patients and it probably wouldn't do them much good emotionally while waiting for an abortion to hear this newly delivered baby crying from an examination room—to say nothing of the spectacle of aide-unit personnel rushing into the clinic.

It all ended well, with the woman delivering in the aide unit on the way to the hospital. She chose to keep the baby and was welcomed with a great outpouring of family support. So it was a happy ending.

But we would have considered it a happy ending if this same woman had come to see us stressing her need to end a pregnancy that could be terminated. We're not here to judge our clients, which places us in marked contrast with the antichoice movement and its persistent inaccuracy in judging the service we provide. Its campaign of disinformation has become increasingly intolerable, especially since what once had been a relatively simple debate has now become an incitement to violence, in recent years leading to the slaughter of health-care providers. For such a developed country America has tolerated persistent disinformation on matters of sex, leading to a general condition in which many haven't a clue what happens after intercourse to cause embryos to grow. Many may believe what was uttered recently by a South Carolina legislator, who opined that rape and abortion are unrelated because "everyone knows" that women can't possibly get pregnant during rape. With so little understanding about basic facts, it isn't difficult to imagine why abortion would carry with it such controversy and mystique.

11

I Can't Be Pregnant Now!

Can a woman really be pregnant to term and not know it? I would have thought not, but the power of denial is extraordinary—even a full-term pregnancy can be denied. At the same time, there are women (particularly younger women and girls) who really have no basis for understanding what pregnancy is. By knowing what it is, we can have a better understanding of what ending it means.

I assume it's understood how pregnancy normally happens, so I'll go beyond the intercourse and fertilization stages. When I teach medical residents, I tell them to think in terms of the size of the uterus. When a normal woman isn't pregnant, the size of her uterus ranges from that of a walnut to a golf ball. I've always taught people to think about three-dimensional objects rather than centimeters when they're doing examinations. When a woman is six-weeks pregnant (counting from the most recent menstrual period), the uterus may be just slightly larger than a golf ball. At eight weeks, it would be similar to the size of a small to medium lemon, though the uterus would feel soft—like relaxed thigh muscles—rather than firm like a lemon. By ten weeks the uterus is the size of a big lemon; at twelve, it's more the size of an orange or a baseball. At fourteen weeks, it's softball- or grapefruit-sized, then on from there.

What's happening is that the conceptus—the fertilized egg— spends many days in transit from the fallopian tube (where it was caught and fertilized) on its way to the uterine wall, where it attaches. The first point at which a sac can be seen and identified by ultrasound is after about four weeks from the most recent menstrual period. At that time a tiny, fuzzy embryonic sac of about ten millimeters in diameter can be seen. The pea-sized sac (placenta) attaches to the uterine wall and, in effect, begins to invade the inner lining of the uterus. The woman's body tends to react to the sac as though it's a foreign object, and consequently the immune system becomes relatively depressed during pregnancy. The placenta appears almost like a tumor as it grows into the wall of the uterus and begins to receive uterine nutrients. By ten weeks it covers one-third to one-half of the interior of the uterus. Then it grows along with the enlargement of the uterus. At term, there's a hormonal change that causes the uterus to begin to contract. The cervix or birth canal dilates and the result is the expulsion of a full-term fetus.

In terminating a pregnancy at any stage, the cervix is artificially dilated from the outside in, and then a suction tube is inserted into the uterus, removing the contents very rapidly. The uterus normally responds by clamping down. When the procedure is done correctly there are one or two drops of blood from the cervix at the end. An abortion can require anywhere from two minutes' worth of suction for a zero-to-nine-week pregnancy to ten or twelve minutes for a woman in her sixteenth week. The safety of the abortion depends on two factors: the healthiness of the uterus and the skill of the provider. The skilled physician is aware when the uterus is empty, when the cervix is not willing to dilate any further, what the wall of a uterus feels like and how it should feel, and whether the procedure caused any holes to be made in the uterus. These are all skills acquired while learning the procedure and working in the field. How risky is the procedure? It has been my experience that those who are doing a good job performing abortions *may* make a hole in the uterus that doesn't require surgery one time in 5,000 cases. A large hole in the uterus requiring surgery might result among some practitioners once in 5,000 procedures. For others, it would be surprising if such a puncture happened once in 20,000 cases.

There's a definite increase in abortion risk starting at seventeen and continuing to nineteen weeks. The risks involve getting amniotic fluid into the maternal bloodstream. Amniotic-fluid embolism is almost universally fatal, but there are safeguards in the procedure to prevent the embolism, or blood-vessel obstruction, from happening. Other risks involve the fact that the instruments are larger for more advanced pregnancies, ones in which uteruses have gotten bigger and uterine walls have gotten thinner. A third risk, called DIC (disseminated intervascular coagulation), affects the clotting factor to such a degree that the patient leaks blood from everywhere. This condition can be very serious. As it happens, fetal skin can be a potent catalyst for DIC, so it's of primary importance that all the contents of the uterus be removed—and removed gently—during the procedure.

Obviously, then, no woman should ever submit to an abortion procedure—if that's the word for it—performed by an unskilled provider. Nonprofessionals (and there were many of them prior to the legalization of abortion) might successfully pull off the procedure, but that success would be more a matter of luck than skill. In any case, today there is no need to seek out some back alley abortionist; despite constant threats to women's reproductive rights, abortion remains a legal and safe procedure when conducted by a qualified practitioner. While there may prove to be fewer practitioners, at least there are enough of us now to see to it that any woman seeking to end an unwanted pregnancy can do so safely.

In the next millennium my prediction is that we will have eliminated at least 50 percent of unwanted pregnancies. We will have done so partly by educating more and more younger people about the use and advantages of the morning-after treatment, which is eminently successful. In addition to the morning after pill, there is drug treatment available during the first trimester, from the moment a woman first thinks she's pregnant until she's four or five weeks pregnant. It's called Methotrexate and has been used for the past few years to treat ectopic pregnancies: those which develop outside the uterus, typically in the fallopian tubes. It also has been shown to work well for intrauterine pregnancies. Consequently, if we can't tell whether the earliest of pregnancies are in the uterus or the fallopian tubes, the woman will use Methotrexate to terminate. For pregnancies through eight or nine weeks we'll be able to use Mifepristone, commonly known by the brand name RU 486. Surgical procedures will also be available through twenty-four weeks.

Women of today can look forward to a time when abortion is more a pharmaceutical than a surgical procedure (we'll discuss the efficacy of Mifepristone at greater length later in this book). It's important, however, to recall that abortion has been legal and acceptable in much of history except for the dark, repressive period of several decades when it was driven underground in this country by small-minded decision-makers, mostly men. That same cabal, playing to the fundamentalists in order to win political favor and get elected to office, is trying its hardest now to consign women to choicelessness. Virtually every state legislative body, emboldened by the so-called Republican landslide of 1994, has attempted to make abortion on demand more difficult. More shameful still has been the reticence from much of the antichoice crowd while doctors and staff members at abortion clinics were being gunned down during the reign of terror of late 1994.

This movement against choice is utterly uninformed about the history of the termination of pregnancies. In fact, abortions predate the times when surgeons were, in effect, no better than blood-letters. Historical documents indicate that abortions by insertion into the uterus and by medication were performed in ancient Egypt, where contraception by condom also was known. In ancient Asia pregnancies were aborted with drugs and with incredibly strong physical manipulation of the uterus. The latter process involved the literal external mashing of the abdomen. It no doubt was a terribly painful procedure that might go on for the better part of an hour until the uterus would contract and there would be a traumatic separation of the placenta from the wall of the uterus.

Why would a woman subject herself to such a procedure? Even to pose the question is to denigrate women and to deny what they have known about themselves for thousands of years. Historically women have known about pregnancy and about the social acceptability of being pregnant at a given time or in specific circumstances. For thousands of years women have taken risks—real or imagined— to avoid or abort pregnancies that they know they can't support. There was, for example, the recent scare about the higher risk of breast cancer among women who have had surgical abortions. But at our clinic we had very few women express any concerns about the reports. Why? Because even if they were true (and other reports indicate that they are not conclusive), women will say: "That's beside the point. I simply can't be pregnant now, and I'm not prepared to deal with any extraneous issues beyond that simple fact." The strength of these women will never cease to amaze me: that they would stare other risks in the face and still choose not to be pregnant. It goes beyond disregard of reports such as the one about breast cancer. Women will avoid even asking about such research because they truly wish to not be dissuaded from ending an unwanted pregnancy.

That's the reality of women's will, and that's why it is sheer folly for the antichoice movement to imagine it ever could legislate away abortion. Yes, it can legislate choice to the point of driving abortion underground again. No, it can never end the resolve women always will have when it comes to making choices that affect their own bodies and their own well-being. Despite the grief and the other emotional responses, the fact is that most women ultimately share a

sense of pride and honor for having dealt positively with an unwanted situation. During the early stages of testing RU 486, it appeared that an obvious hypothesis could be made: Women feel even
more positive about ending an unwanted pregnancy when the abortion procedure involves drugs rather than surgery. Perhaps they find
it more "natural," though I'm not sure how the taking of pills is more
natural than the insertion of a small piece of tubing. The lay sense
seems to be that Mifepristone and Misoprostol not only mean a simpler procedure but a less intrusive one: that whatever the body is
doing, it's doing so on its own.

If so (and we'll examine this in greater depth), then such control would be in marked contrast to the status quo for much of this
century. As always happens when governments drive abortions underground, a certain percentage of the medical establishment responds heroically. Certain doctors come forward at great risk to their
medical licenses, their well-being, and even their freedom so that
they can be available to provide safe abortions for women who might
otherwise seek the procedure through dubious, perhaps deadly
means. This very honorable group is to be contrasted with those who
realize that desperate people will pay anything to be relieved of the
source of their desperation. When abortion is driven underground,
there's an immediate proliferation of unskilled and, frankly, very
evil people to take advantage of desperate women. The stories of the
abortion underground that prevailed until a quarter century ago are
hair-raising, and must be utterly unbelievable to a generation of
young women who have enjoyed the freedom (albeit a freedom constantly challenged) to control their own reproductive lives. There
are tales of having to take a taxi to one place; thereupon being dispatched in another taxi; arriving at yet another place; heading up
the stairs, through an apartment, around a corner to another room,
with dried blood, bad odors, dim light, dirty "surgical" equipment,
and unsympathetic and unskilled practitioners waiting to take a
huge sum of money to perform the painful work that results in pools
of blood at best, slow death at worst. There is absolutely no evidence

anywhere to suggest that making abortion illegal will result in anything but the killing of more women. The antichoice movement likes to believe that outlawing abortions would reduce the number of procedures. All it ever reduces is the number of procedures that are reported. Then again, perhaps that's enough to mollify the antichoice crowd. Maybe it's enough for them to drive abortion underground, the hope being that if it isn't reported then it somehow has gone away. It's the ostrich assumption: out of sight, out of mind. But it must be extremely difficult for antichoice people to feel that they've held the moral high ground if outlawing abortion results in the death of a lot of women.

On the other hand, let it be recalled that the death rate of women having abortions went to nearly zero after abortion was legalized. Abortion is one of the safest of all surgical procedures. As we know from National Abortion Federation statistics, there is a sixfold greater risk of a woman dying while giving birth than succumbing during an abortion. But prior to legalization, as many women died during abortion procedures as during childbirth. Do we have the ideal now that abortion is legal in the United States? No, because the world beyond this country remains a perilous place for women with unwanted pregnancies. The organizations to which I belong estimate that, worldwide, a woman dies every three minutes from a botched abortion. But let's say the woman doesn't die during an abortion procedure performed by someone unskilled. Think of the other consequences of nonlethal but botched abortions. Tissue may be left behind. Whatever instrumentation is used may not be handled carefully enough to see to it that (a) the uterus is emptied completely, and/or (b) the uterus doesn't wind up with a big hole in it, and/or (c) the cervix isn't split. So let's pose a best-case scenario under which a woman getting an unprofessional abortion somehow manages to survive totally intact and somehow miraculously is among the 10 percent who don't get an infection under such circumstances. That leaves 90 percent of women who undergo such a procedure under dubious circumstances with cervixes that don't work anymore because they've been dilated too forcefully or torn. They're subject to terrible infections and they run the risk of eventually bleeding to death because of holes in their uteruses that expose blood vessels. Or, if tissue is left in the uterus, the resulting bleeding can be horrendous, because tissue that remains embedded in the uterine walls prevents the blood vessels which supplied that area of tissue from closing. Therefore they are forced to remain open, pumping blood dangerously into the uterine cavity, hence the very real stories about women dying in pools of blood. The vessels pumping blood to the uterus are so big and strong that if a woman is improperly cared for she can die amazingly fast.

So where does a scared eighteen-year-old summon the wherewithal to go through the scenario I've described? Intellectually I know that her courage comes from plain desperation. She simply can't envision her life after carrying the pregnancy to term and she will, evidently, do anything to end it. But the act of obtaining a clandestine abortion under dubious conditions must be something like jumping into an unlit abyss. Yet, there were untold thousands of American women driven to such extremes. Of course, there was also the attendant double standard in this country. While women of lesser means would be forced for socioeconomic reasons to seek the back-alley abortion solution, there were the wives and daughters of well-heeled families whose physicians either could be persuaded to perform the procedure safely or who could recommend a proper clinic on foreign soil.

But isn't that usually the social reality in the United States? Isn't there always the double standard about "them" and "us"? Leaders speak in platitudes about standards of behavior, but when they condemn behavior they're really talking about something that "other" people are doing. Or perhaps they make exceptions for those who are near and dear to themselves. Newt Gingrich and many of his lockstep sympathizers have in the past been unrestrained in their criticism, for example, of the gay lifestyle. But Gingrich, for one, lately has stopped short of further criticism (much less condemnation) of gays because of the public acknowledgment by his own half-sister that she is a lesbian. Phyllis Schlafly, similarly, is in league with unabashed homophobes, the exception to her own professed abhorrence of the gay lifestyle being the behavior of her own son, who is gay.

And so it becomes all right in many antichoice circles to qualify what "anti" means. What it actually means to many who say they oppose abortion is that the procedure should not be allowed for "them." But what if Ms. Schlafly or Ms. Gingrich or Ms. Dole or Ms. Gramm or their close friends should experience an unwanted pregnancy? Put another way: Are we genuinely to believe that none of the antichoice leaders past or present is related to or knows a woman who has chosen to have an abortion? With women's reproductive rights yet again representing a major election-year issue, would every antichoice candidate be willing to go on record pledging that nobody he or she knows and loves ever had one? My assumption is that the answer is no. These leaders know a lot of women. They must know at least one who at some time in her life chose to end an unwanted pregnancy. If so, then would that candidate seriously have wished that such a woman subject herself to an unsafe abortion? Do the rules apply equally to the powerful and the wealthy? Well, the rules didn't apply equally when abortion was illegal, because then the wealthy and well-connected women still managed to take care of matters safely, if discreetly.

What would I be doing had I been practicing medicine when abortions were illegal? I will say with all honesty that I am more hesitant with my response now than I might have been a few years ago, before many of my peers were being stalked and, as we see on several recent solemn occasions, shot and wounded or killed for what they do. But I still can say that I probably would have been part of a women's underground health collective, helping perform abortions for women rich and poor while maintaining a regular practice. And I'd also be one of the doctors who would be training lay practitioners to do the procedure. Properly trained lay practitioners, after all, did a great job during the years prior to legalization. They came up with innovative methods that probably helped improve the procedure after abortion rights were legalized. But I have to say that it has become a considerable challenge in light of violent developments of recent years to paint a brave face on coming to work every day. The pride definitely exists and it always will. The commitment hasn't waned and it won't. The daily honoring of women who make the hard choice to keep control of their bodies and lives: That remains a vital reason to go to work every day. But I would be much less than candid if I denied that the violent turn taken by the anti-choice movement hasn't given me pause.

I can recall fondly, for example, having started a journal intended for my sons to read when they reach the age at which they can appreciate such things. The first entry is from November 15, 1985. Until recently, I didn't quite grasp why I abruptly stopped writing in the book after January 1993. During the final entry I allude to the optimism that attended that month: "George Bush is no longer the President as of Jan. 20," I wrote. "Bill Clinton takes over, and I hope to write later on of the fulfillment of at least some of the dreams of peace, equality of women, respect for children, and more sharing of wealth in our country."

Such egalitarian wishes persist in me. But, as I say, the journal entries stopped abruptly in January 1993. Lately I've come to appreciate that it has to do with something else that happened that month. January 1993 also was when a colleague was gunned down for no reason other than the fact that he was performing perfectly legal, honorable medical procedures. His murder was an act of unimaginable cowardice and hypocrisy that immediately altered the entire calculus of what was meant by being an abortion doctor. But it also posed a direct challenge to the very idea of being a feminist in this country. It was an act of terrorism that declared open, unabated warfare on my profession, and it abruptly destroyed much of the optimism that had sustained me since the heady months of our family sabbatical in Europe.

12

The Struggle That Remains

The optimism I had felt prior to early 1992 is apparent from my journal entries. Thousands of parents no doubt have, as I did, found it therapeutic from a personal standpoint and potentially valuable for children to keep a diary or journal. The prose of mine, I'm afraid, has been as florid at times as the rose-and-posey cloth cover of the journal. Something so heartfelt necessarily lends itself to such rapturous departures, and of course I make no apologies for them.

Perhaps it's worth recalling the spirit with which the journal was begun. I think the initial entry may speak universally to the joy and wonder parents feel when they recognize what a gift it is to have wanted children.

"It's hard to begin a book such as this," I wrote on November 15, 1985, "and I can make no guarantees that I'll write in it every day. I will write as often as I can and hope to make this more a patchwork of feelings than a time chronicle. You two are the most dramatic and important things that have ever happened to me and your dad. There are absolutely no moments in life that resemble the incredible high and surge of protectiveness that we felt at each of your births. It was overwhelming joy coupled with an enormous sense of awe that we had done this together and a very real and scary sense of how responsible we were, to and for you. These feelings are all still there, but the love has deepened and grown as we've watched you become such distinct little persons."

Amid the journal entries are numerous personal anecdotes. But I find that I paused now and then to reflect about political matters. Such was the case on November 13, 1988, when I wrote: "I feel as though the forces of darkness have won a round! Mike Dukakis and Lloyd Bentsen were soundly defeated (51 to 49 percent) by Bush and Quayle (son of John Birch Society card-carrying members); three antichoice ballot measures passed in Colorado, Arkansas and Michigan, and once again the white-male society dominates. It is never popular to be for the dispossessed and disenfranchised—maybe your generation. . . . We've had wonderfully interesting discussions about the candidates and their positions during this election time, and the two of you came with me while I voted. You will certainly be politically aware as you grow."

I went on to note how my oldest son had given "a whole week's allowance to Puget Sound Sane because you felt it was so important to work to prevent nuclear war. You are wonderful little boys who are hopefully growing up with a more flexible view of the world—kinder and gentler."

The latter expression I somehow passed along without noting the irony of it having been Bush's campaign theme. That irony was implicit, however, in a later journal entry: "As a personal aside, I'm finally reading *The Feminine Mystique*, and although it's almost twenty years old now it remains disturbingly accurate. We seem to live in a time of great societally approved hostility to women: rape, domestic violence, child sexual abuse, extreme poverty for divorced women and their children, threats to reproductive rights, much lower pay for women than for men and renewed talk of women gratefully retiring to hearth and children, of the need for 'Mommy' tracks to somehow justify holding women back and a president who shows the way by keeping his own wife psychologically muzzled. The struggle continues. You will undoubtedly help by being thoughtful feminist males."

It wasn't long after that entry that we decided to take the sabbatical. Upon returning, John and I were feeling tremendously good about the future, vowing to take back the lessons we observed from friends in Europe: take more days off together, spend more time at family pursuits, deemphasize materialism—in short: simplify our lives. We kept that up—I think to our credit—for almost a year.

It was during that time that I was elected to the board of the National Abortion Federation (NAF), which is the only national professional organization that supports, educates, and trains abortion providers. For nearly twenty years it's been a membership organization composed of various clinics and doctors who provide abortion services. The mission statement of the NAF is to assure access to and quality of abortion through teaching. Lately we're moving toward setting standards for abortion care in the United States. The organization, in any case, started with fewer than a dozen members and now has some 350. Member doctors and clinics provide about half the abortions done in the country.

After joining NAF and attending my initial meetings at the Washington, D.C., headquarters, I began to rise in the organization. Here was this outspoken female physician among mostly men. During my first visits I'd be one of maybe three women, though that number has grown steadily until now it's more like three dozen female physicians in attendance. When I was elected to the board there had never been a woman in such a position. This might very well have seemed odd at the time, but it needed to be placed into proper context. In truth, I wasn't finding omissions of women odd at that point of my feminism because women hadn't yet emerged in medicine in any great numbers. It was obvious from national contacts I had made that most of the well-known providers in America were men. Women who had just begun coming to medical schools during the 1970s were aware that it takes time to establish oneself professionally before becoming a major abortion provider. As I write this, there are now two female physicians on the board, and we're trying to recruit more women. One obstacle is financial. The NAF board is a pay-as-you-go proposition, so it probably costs in excess of $3,000 per year in expenses for a member to serve. It also requires having a fairly stable clinic because of the time it takes to be away from work attending meetings and staying involved.

Some understandably confuse the NAF with NARAL. The former is strictly an educational organization for the providers, whereas the National Abortion Rights Action League (NARAL)* is a political and public-education group. At NAF we have two annual meetings, one focusing on skills and the other on risk management. Lectures are given by providers from around the country. As far as skills go, somebody might speak about, say, ultrasound care; another might address emotional care and counseling techniques or the business aspect of keeping a clinic going. So in this way NAF appeals to all layers of the provider system. The risk-management aspect involves case discussions: difficult cases, emergency situations, and the like.

Does NAF overlap with the work of NARAL and other political groups? As a practical matter it's imperative that we do, especially in view of solidifying our mutual opposition to challenges to reproductive rights. We have to maintain contact if only to keep political groups informed about what's acceptable procedure and what isn't. There are bills being introduced and laws being passed that may prompt some to say: "Oh, I'm sure this would be okay with the providers." But it decidedly is not okay. Legal encroachment on fundamental rights is never okay. NARAL, in any case, is the only exclusive reproductive-rights advocacy group, but it obviously isn't the only organization devoted to keeping abortions available and safe. The National Organization for Women is another. The Fund

---

*Recently renamed the National Abortion and Reproductive Rights Action League.

for the Feminist Majority is a third. While the issue of abortion rights takes precedence in virtually any feminist discussion, it scarcely is the only subject that occupies these groups. Even NARAL is now moving to a more general emphasis, including family-planning and health-care-reform issues.

When I speak of encroachments, I refer both to overt and subtle ways of curbing the reality of abortion availability. The following example will serve to illustrate. Back in 1986, at the beginning of the picketing troubles that were experienced by some providers, a doctor here got involved with one of the protesters in front of his clinic. During the confrontation the doctor supposedly knocked some papers out of the picketer's arms and was accused of assault. To prevent such confrontations in our area, we formed the Washington State Abortion Providers' Organization. The doctors involved decided to make it an organization independent of the state NARAL group. We became, then, a sort of mini-NAF for the state, offering support, education and information-sharing for all providers. In its capacity as a state advocacy group for choice, NARAL agreed to provide the staffing for our organization. The arrangement was that our members would pay to belong, with part of that money going toward paying for the staffing from NARAL. That arrangement has worked out quite well. In 1988, for example, we began to hear of a lot of trouble with insurance malpractice rates. Suddenly providers found their malpractice rates going up after performing a certain number of abortions. The same was true for performing a second-trimester abortion, unless it was done in a hospital. In short, the insurance companies had taken it upon themselves to make these groundless decisions that were inflating our premium rates. That prompted us to form a task force, which included a couple of lawyers, doctors, and administrators from some of the clinics. We put together some factual information: a perfect example of how activists, providers, and attorneys can work together to make something happen. The lawyers, in any case, pulled all our information together and presented it to the insurance companies. Our complaint to the insur-

ance industry dragged on for a couple of years, but it was finally resolved. It resulted in changing the rate system, and also led to the
agreement that there was absolutely no medical reason not to do second-trimester abortions in clinics.

Because of the concessions we were able to win, our state task
force became a tremendous resource for provider groups in other
states facing similar obstacles. We learned how much more secure we
could be if we made the effort to get together and help one another
with mutual problems rather than try to compete. But Washington
is an unusual state in this regard. It's extremely rare for a state to
maintain local provider organizations. The status quo in many states,
sad to say, is an adversary relationship between certain providers.
This scarcely addresses the compelling issue of reproductive rights:
the rights themselves. In any case, Washington's leadership no doubt
had a lot to do with me being elected to the board of NAF. Providers
from other parts of the country always seem to listen wistfully to
Washington success stories. This relates directly to the fact that
physicians in this state who have been doing the greatest numbers
of abortions have been well respected in the medical community for
years. They've never been what could be called "sideline" doctors on
political issues. Washington itself has traditionally been a prochoice
state, though the Republican majority of the state house of representatives, emboldened by what it considered its mandate from November 1994, has attempted repeatedly to curb reproductive rights.
Members of the GOP do so even while admitting in newspaper reports that such legislative proposals have no chance of sustaining
state senate scrutiny, much less finding favor with any gubernator-
ial leadership the state has had during the past twenty years. Washington, at least until recently, has been a more or less live-and-let-
live place where the rights of the individual are concerned. Such
fear- and hate-mongering tactics as antigay ballot initiatives have repeatedly failed here, even while neighboring Oregon—itself normally a bastion of individual rights and civility—saw such a measure
go to a general vote. Not to wave any red flags, but it must be noted

that even Washington's antichoice crowd by and large has been much less hostile than in other well-reported parts of the country. The western Washington community in particular is one of the most tolerant places in America. I knew this twenty years ago when I arrived to begin my family practice residencies in Seattle.

Obviously not all areas of the country are as relatively respectful of women's reproductive rights as Washington State. Where would I least prefer to be an abortion provider? Based on several reasons, three places: Florida, Mississippi and Missouri. The reasons include extreme hostility to abortion providers, the lack of political support for abortion rights, and the extreme isolation of abortion providers. Louisiana's not great, either, though I do have friends who are working there as providers. Then again, antichoice spectacles in New Orleans may have made America at large wonder if Louisiana is to be the next Florida with respect to public protests.

Even given Washington State's relatively enlightened views on reproductive rights, I envision a time when I no longer will be a provider. I will leave in my place a lot of well-trained abortion practitioners, but my husband and I know from our European sabbatical that we will eventually leave the work to others. In Europe we began to ask ourselves basic questions about our own lives and careers. I imagine most normal people, no matter how intense they are about their life's work, ask themselves the same things: How long, for example, would we need to keep working until we could retire to a less hectic life? Until then, what would be my level of prochoice involvement? Beyond retirement what would I do? It remains unanswered, though the day will come when I'll have to decide.

The struggle for reproductive rights remains in the here and now. And it seems that the fight presents more obstacles every time providers turn around. During the late 1980s, for example, the availability of intrauterine contraceptive devices (IUDs) started decreasing. Along with the spectacle of ever more vocal protests, the lack of IUDs represented what seems in retrospect to have been the beginning of prochoice troubles coming from all sides. But I wasn't about to sit back and watch as IUD availability declined. I began buying up IUDs every time I went to Canada. There you could pick them up at any pharmacy with a prescription from a physician. Canada was enlightened about the value of the IUD in direct proportion to the shortsightedness in the United States. It was as though what my mother always said about the social superiority of Canada were only too true. The quality of the Canadian IUDs was precisely the same as the ones here had been, but they sold up north for a tenth the U.S. price (and why shouldn't they be relatively inexpensive when you consider how little labor or raw material goes into the device?). Anyway, I considered buying up the Canadian product to be a real coup, and I did the same thing with the birth-control-injection drug Depoprovera. Unfortunately, espionage on the part of an American IUD supplier led to a threat to expose my importation of contraceptive devices from Canada. The supplier wrote a letter stating more or less that it was aware I'd been dispensing IUDs, but since I hadn't bought any from that particular company it was obvious I must be bringing them in from elsewhere. The threat was that the supplier was going to turn me in to the Food and Drug Administration. I will grant that the supplier had a point: The device I was bringing in had never been tested and passed by the FDA of this country. On the other hand, it was precisely the same as the one from the U.S. supplier. The difference? About $300. Where the Canadian device cost about $30, the U.S. brand ran more than ten times as much, and I was able to pass along the savings to my patients.

Why would any person or group suddenly single out my clinic for harassment? Possibly because we had become higher profile. When I began devoting all my attention to the clinic, my name started appearing in various newspapers and periodicals. I spoke on radio and television. Where once we enjoyed the sort of obscurity in which a little clinic can do a lot to benefit women, now we were much more noticeable. When that happens, you have to live with the idea that you've become a much more conspicuous threat. Now that we were "exposed" for having taken humane cost-cutting measures for the benefit of our patients, some of the other economic steps we'd taken had to be abandoned. We'd always, for example, saved money and passed it along by reusing so-called disposable tissue-waste plastic cannulas (the small plastic tube which is inserted into a woman's uterus to empty it during her abortion). We even had a long-standing arrangement with a hospital that would accept our used cannulas, then gas-sterilize them and allow us to reuse them rather than disposing of them. That in itself would negate an environmentally wasteful practice. In the nineties, suddenly abortion was being scrutinized much more widely. One day we got a letter from the hospital informing us that it no longer was willing to continue the cleaning and recycling arrangement. It was obvious when we looked into it that the hospital had felt pressure of becoming a party in some potential malpractice suit involving us. The result is that we now go through four times the plastic cannulas that we did during the years when sterilization of the containers allowed us to reuse them three times.

Government regulation of abortion clinics can indeed be subtle. We looked into saving costs by installing our own gas-sterilization system. It was deemed impossible because we lacked the proper number of exhaust fans. Could the exhaust fans be installed? No, there were other reasons why this was impossible. Could we at least pay to see to it that the cannulas somehow could get sterilized so that they could be given away to needy Third World clinics? Absolutely not. We wanted to use Depoprovera, but had to jump through various agency hoops because the drug hadn't been approved specifically for birth control. Never mind that it had been okayed as a drug to be prescribed by any licensed physician with good intentions. But wasn't I just that, a licensed physician? Then why the hassle? Eventually we were allowed to keep prescribing the drug, but only after trading a number of letters with government agencies. How did the government find out to begin with about my prescribing Depoprovera? We don't know. We can only assume there was a tip-off from the antichoice group.

We don't like being told on by antichoice-zealots, especially when our actions are intended to provide quality care at the least cost to the client. It would be terrific if our clinic somehow could return to the state of anonymity we enjoyed for so many years. Our approach at every juncture has been to do what it takes to be the most squeaky clean clinic imaginable. For example, because of the retirement of some nearby providers, it became necessary for us during the early 1990s to extend care beyond what had been our thirteen-week pregnancy limit. We increased the limit to sixteen weeks, meaning we would do second-trimester procedures. I began my training in such procedures, using NAF and other educational resources. As it happened, we needed to be reinspected by the state in order to be licensed to go beyond the first trimester. The state visited and pronounced us the best-organized clinic it had ever seen. But then there was subsequent involvement by another state agency, a relatively new bureaucracy supposedly charged with assuring laboratory quality for outpatients. As a practical matter, what it meant was paying the state $500 a year for the privilege of having lab procedures and equipment inspected. It also meant spending untold hours writing up protocols, providing more documentation, and spending yet another $1,000 a year being tested by yet another pathology lab.

During the past five years, then, it's as though providers have heard what amounts to a growing cacophony of side-issue noise. The message, which is getting louder all the time, is: Be careful, don't take any economic shortcuts, because you're under constant surveillance by the antichoice forces.

Economic shortcuts can make eminent good sense when viewed away from the hysteria of antichoice incantations. Let's consider, for example, a possible, practical shortcut to tissue disposal. Realistically, the best and safest way medically to dispose of tissue from the uterus is to put it directly into the general sewage system. Waste of every kind, after all, eventually winds up being disposed of in one manner or another, and short of sacred burial rites it's safe to say that disposal of organic matter (which uterine tissue is) is generally a fairly straightforward proposition. The matter leftover from surgery is all natural tissue and blood. Could it be infected? Yes, and that's why the best place for it is the sewage system, where it will get dispersed, treated, and disinfected. Eventually all molecules reunite in other ways and make up new compounds. Because no matter is ever created or destroyed, the fact is inescapable that even the most sacred of matter eventually is recycled into the world so that any one of us at any time might contain molecular material that once was part of a plant or a stone or a whatever.

So the disposal of human tissue differs not at all from the disposal of any other material. But an obvious problem is presented when considering that larger pieces of tissue can block disposal pipes. The logical solution, then, would be to reduce large tissue with a disposal grinder. After all, waste tissue eventually is reduced and decays no matter what the method of disposal. Aesthetically, of course, some have trouble with the idea of disposing of human tissue.

Such was the case with the plumber we asked to come and install a disposal system on our premises. He went into the room and went to work. But before the work was finished my colleague found the poor man on the floor literally sobbing at the thought of a disposal system at a health clinic. He immediately reported us to the county health department, which led to a series of opinions about the requisite dimensions for disposable human tissue, including one opinion that "you simply cannot reduce the size of tissue before disposing of it."

We're left, then, with a disposal system that sits where it is, never used. Because the original plumber couldn't bring himself to complete the work, we wound up hiring a prochoice woman plumber to finish the job. But that isn't the end of it, of course. The tissue still must be sent through the reclamation process. So we keep it, freeze it, and pass it off periodically to a disposal company, which takes it somewhere and incinerates it. Or maybe, for all we know, they run it through a disposal system similar to the one we spent so much time and money to install.

As a result, we foster a kind of offshoot industry, providing work for disposers of tissue because of regulations that grow more absurd in direct proportion to the influence the antichoice crowd wields with conservative decision-makers. Where does it end? We don't know yet. We do know that the aesthetic displeasure of one uninformed plumber can cause all sorts of regulatory hassles. What also seems clear is that quasi-legal regulatory obstacles scarcely present the only source of protest from the antichoice circle. Lately the stakes have been raised beyond the levels of rage and outrage, as I reluctantly conceded one day when I found myself looking for something to wear to work. It would have been a nice distraction, too, had I been looking for a cloth jacket instead of being fitted for a bulletproof vest.

13

Terror

There is nothing amusing about the notion of women finding themselves in need of dealing with unwanted pregnancies. Nothing in my experience suggests any levity whatsoever, even if the spectacle of a plumber on his knees sobbing about a garbage disposal might conjure a scene from some dark comic opera.

I hasten to add here that this man is one who might have benefited from asking a few logical questions. Instead of assuming that somehow we are in the business of murdering babies, he might have taken the trouble to ask us. We then could have said to him: "Here, this is a bowl of tissue that has resulted from an abortion operation. It's tissue not unlike the stuff leftover from any operation. It contains organic material that once was living but now is not living. It was tissue contained in a woman who made a conscious decision that she no longer wanted this tissue in her body. You can feel free to regard this tissue in any way you choose. But the fact remains that you have no claim on this tissue, and neither does anybody else in the world except for the one woman who was pregnant but who chose not to be pregnant anymore."

The plumber's reaction illustrates the aura of great mystery surrounding what goes on at my clinic and others. Whatever it was that the plumber imagined happens there led to yet another go-around with the health department, yet another obstacle (and in fact a restriction) to the work we do.

So the grief-stricken plumber reports my clinic to the health department, whereupon yet another person becomes appalled at the idea of little embryos being sent down a garbage disposal. The result is that the health department decrees that no human tissue can be made smaller for the purpose of disposal. Never mind that we could find nothing in health-department regulations that indicated such a rule. Just so that I can stay in business, operating a clinic in today's climate has meant going the extra distance at every juncture to see that every regulation is met whether it exists on paper or merely in the mind of a health-department bureaucrat. "Don't make tissue smaller!" That was the order. And we knew we'd be inspected anyway, if only for the fact that we were performing second-trimester abortions. We could have, I suppose, gone ahead and used the disposal anyway, but then I might have been forcing my staff to lie eventually to some health inspector. That's the last thing in the world I would do. We're trying for honesty and openness here with the hope that the opposition someday will strive for the same. So the only comedy in all this derives from the absurdities that arise when regulations become restrictions. Yet, I've been making a lot of practical decisions about the clinic by saying to myself: Look, this makes absolutely no sense medically; it's costing a lot of extra money, but I'm going to do it anyway and be done with it.

In the past, I'll admit, I may have defied certain regulations by allowing a woman to take home with her the placenta and tissue after an operation. It was my practice to remind such women that they needed to dispose of the tissue in a timely fashion because it degenerates quickly. But, after all, it is their tissue. It came from them;

it belongs to them. Yet certain regulations are such that a woman wishing to own the tissue taken from her body during an operation must be licensed to take it away from the medical office. Such regulations don't necessarily extend to all tissue. If I removed gall stones, for example, my patient could take them home with her. But abortion tissue? No. Maybe it's because certain official factions of society feel the public somehow has a claim not only on a woman's reproductive rights but on the very tissue inside her uterus.

Are such procedural obstacles true restrictions to a woman's right to choose to end an unwanted pregnancy? Do they amount to harassment? Are they just the typical hassles that are encountered by any overregulated business? I don't think the latter is true. During the past half decade abortion clinics have been regulated out of existence in some cases. Even after a Washington State ballot initiative called for slackening regulations for most businesses, moves were afoot to find ways around the language of the initiative so that the state could keep hassling abortion clinics. One of the top priorities of the conservative majority of the Washington state legislature, elected during the so-called 1994 landslide, was weakening a state law that guarantees abortion rights for all women. One bill would have cut funding for poor women seeking to end unwanted pregnancies. Another would have seen to it that young women would have to notify parents two days before getting an abortion. The latter idea sounded terrific to the conservative members of the state house. Then a Seattle Democrat decided she would test her colleagues' resolve by offering an amendment. Instead of just notifying parents of the pregnant young woman, she proposed also notifying the parents of the male party to the pregnancy. During floor debate one legislator spoke of how difficult it might be determining the sperm donor—the potential father. This idea, ironically, is near the crux of the prochoice position. Because many young men (and a lot of older men) feel they can impregnate women with impunity, the burden of bearing the responsibility for a pregnancy and a child falls upon the woman. This strengthens the argument that it is the woman's right to decide what to do about the pregnancy. The state house, in any case, passed the amended bill, with sponsors fully aware that the legislation never would go anywhere—which it didn't.

Somehow my clinic has been surprisingly resistant to every encroachment. We've jumped through every regulation hoop. We've emerged clean from every inspection. While there is a downturn in the number of abortions in the country, our clinic actually has shown a steady increase in patients. Moreover, we have shown national leadership in a number of ways, the most recent of which was in testing Mifepristone, results of which will be shared in later chapters.

Prior to that we were one of the first clinics to become certified to insert Norplant implants, Norplant being the long-term birth-control method that is positioned under the skin and lasts for several years. During the first year, we held repeated seminars on the procedure, training hundreds in the process. I personally got involved with Wyeth, the pharmaceutical company that distributes Norplant. It will be another year or two before we'll be able to gauge all the effects of the original Norplant insertions, which were made during quite a flurry of interest in 1991 and 1992. Women were coming into our clinic at a rate of about six a month for the procedure, which involves the insertion of six small capsules that contain a measured amount of progesterone that is released slowly into the bloodstream. The substance reduces the number of ovulations. Plus, women with Norplant insertions don't get pregnant because the procedure results in changes in cervical mucus as well uterine lining. It also alters the motility of the fallopian tubes by causing the small hairlike structures called ciliae in the tubes which normally beat within the tube and carry the eggs toward to uterus to slow or even reverse direction. Before this procedure we never were able to look at contraception over such a lengthy period as the five-year Norplant term. The failure rate, in any case, is less than 1 percent during the first few years and seems to be no higher than 2 percent in the final years of the insertion. This is minuscule when compared to other forms of birth control. It makes Norplant nothing less than a fabulous means of birth control because it allows women to get on with their lives without having to worry about maintenance or mistakes. The downside of Norplant is that it costs about $500 (in 1995 dollars) to have the capsules put in and another $200 to have them taken out. Most of the initial cost of about $400 is for the capsules themselves. Another danger is that Norplant is a procedure that can't be ended without involving a physician. It isn't the same, for example, as simply deciding to quit taking birth-control pills or opting to toss out the diaphragm.

Then there's the more sinister side of the Norplant procedure. The question has been raised in some authoritarian circles that the insertions ought to be part of the punitive process involving, say, women who are crack-cocaine addicts, to wit: "You've broken the law, so now we're going to see to it that you can't get pregnant anymore." A similar argument involves poor women, including the classic "welfare mother" popularized by conservatives: "You've had too many babies, so we're going to see to it you can't have anymore." In this way, Norplant insertions could become Newt Gingrich's perfect alternative to the much maligned notion of dragging off the children of poor people and warehousing them in orphanages. Whether a woman's "crime," in any case, is deemed by society to be drug abuse or poverty, the reasoning about a Norplant "solution" proceeds from the notion that women's reproductive rights somehow belong to the state (belong, here again, in the same sense that the very tissue extracted from uterine operations is state-controlled property). Using Norplant as punishment raises yet another question of sexual fairness. What would male America say about a political hierarchy that insisted men must—or must not—father children under given circumstances? What if the government in effect said: "You've been convicted of several crimes and have proven yourself to be the kind of man who impregnates women and abandons them. Ergo, we're going to insert under your skin a drug that sterilizes you." Or: "You live in poverty, and therefore we're going to insist you undergo vasectomy." How many men—and what organization of men—

would sit still for that kind of government control over their sexual functions? By posing such hypotheticals, maybe we can see more clearly the direction such reasoning takes us when society shows a willingness to make reproductive-rights decisions for individuals.

Despite its potential for abuse, Norplant has proven to be an excellent birth-control method for many women. It obviously requires a long-term commitment, but it serves as yet another example of the relative extremes to which women are willing to go to gain and maintain control of their own reproductive capacities. We have observed elsewhere in this book the groundless argument that certain women are somehow less deserving of abortion rights than others. The less-deserving would be those who repeatedly get pregnant: abortion recidivists I guess is what the antichoice crowd would call them. One might ask how a person could, in effect, use up her rights to something. But even if it were true (and I have no evidence that it is), that there were a lot of women repeatedly getting pregnant and seeking repeated abortions, then wouldn't it make more sense for physicians to be able to make Norplant available in such cases?

By late 1993, I had become convinced that the threats to women's reproductive rights by the antichoice camp had escalated to a new level. The shooting of a Florida colleague demonstrated to me that a horrible barrier had been broken. Until then I had said, and with great faith, "the antichoice zealots will lock your doors, they'll put themselves in front of your car, and do all kinds of incredibly annoying, harassing things, but they'd never hurt anybody." I conceded that the opposition was doing as it was entitled to do: using First Amendment rights of protest and free speech, contesting what they consider to be untenable. Fine, I thought. It's incredibly irritating, but that's the way it is. Women have a legal right to choose in this country; the antichoice side has the legal right to want to deny freedom of choice. All of us who are providers, I think, felt there genuinely was a barrier beyond which nobody from the other side would go. They wouldn't actually hurt anybody. Even if they bombed clinics, they did so when there was nobody there. But the killing of Dr. David Gunn in Florida was the most horrible development imaginable.

Some in my field seemed at the time to rationalize the murder as some kind of isolated, crackpot incident. It was something confined to such flashpoint areas as Pensacola and would never happen again, much less spread. If nothing else, the more moderating voices amid the antichoice hierarchy would condemn such violence as they had condemned the clinic bombings of the eighties. They would, as it were, take care of their own. It would never happen again.

That was in early 1993. Then, during the summer, a half hour after I finished talking with him on the phone, Dr. George Tiller of Wichita, Kansas, was shot in both arms. We'd been talking about RU 486. He and I had become acquainted at national meetings of the National Abortion Federation. His was one of the rare clinics doing third-trimester abortions for women with terrible fetal anomalies, whose fetuses have severe and life-threatening deformities or chromosomal abnormalities. A skilled family physician, he also is such a close acquaintance that the savage attack made me realize how vulnerable I'd become. This seemed especially the case since the woman who shot him was from Portland, Oregon, just two hundred miles to the south. Such proximity put the threat in my own back yard. No longer was I left with any intellectual protection. I couldn't say to myself: "This will only happen to people I don't know or who live a continent away." Also, the Tiller shooting meant that violence no longer was an isolated phenomenon.

For, unbeknownst to me, the antichoice fringe at the time already was publishing and circulating the nefarious *Army of God* handbook, one of the most horrifying collections of writing ever circulated. A photocopied version of this vile document came into our possession, and we keep it at the office. It's anonymously written, possibly by a number of antichoice fringe types. It not only advocates the murder or maiming of abortion providers and the bombing and obstruction of clinics, it also spells out how to accomplish such obviously illegal—to say nothing of immoral—objectives.

This is a manual full of quasi-biblical references and anti-Clinton—or "Klinton," as in "Klinton's Amerika"—paranoia. A "revised and expanded" edition carries a box titled "Legal Stuff," apparently intended as some sort of disclaimer. It reads: "Slick Willie and Company . . . would love to put the person who sold or gave you this book in jail. So—just for the record: The information contained in this book is intended solely for the interest and/or amusement of, and what it may be worth to, the reader for information purposes only. It is not intended to encourage the activities mentioned and described therein."

In fact, the manual goes on through dozens of rambling pages to advocate nothing less than violence against life and property. It purports to proceed from Christian teachings while offering nothing but unmitigated hatred. It revels in paranoid jokes and juvenile noms de guerre. The authors speak of being at "war," summoning zealous language that sounds like Pat Buchanan at his most divisive. Those of us who are prochoice are demonized or described as, for example, "dope-sucking, child-molesting, homosexual atheists." The performing of disruptive pranks or violent crimes is dismissed as no worse from a moral standpoint than posting a bogus "Beware of Dog" sign to put off would-be burglars. Suggestions about "Ninety-nine covert ways to stop abortion" are facetiously attributed to Margaret Sanger and Faye Wattleton. Disruptions include gluing shut the locks at abortion clinics and causing traffic snarls with "park-ins." Elaborate schemes involving concrete read as though they've been dreamed up by some bygone conference of juvenile delinquents. Much is made of the disruptive possibilities of water or refuse sent through mail drops. Cutting phone lines and other service conduits is advocated. Ruses involving HIV testing are proposed.

None of the above is so surprising after witnessing the disruptions to clinics during the 1980s. One can but imagine how much better served the country would be if those who contributed to this remarkably hateful piece of literature had instead spent the time helping poor children get food or education. But, here again, the antichoice movement always has been pointedly silent on the notion of concern for the already born. Indeed, until it became all right to speak aloud about sentencing poor kids to orphanages, about the only context in which children of poverty were mentioned by conservatives in this country was in terms of the social burden they bring to bear.

The manual's sections about disruption gradually lead to tutorials about explosives. What must truly alarm law-enforcers, however, are the manual's sequences about stalking, maiming and murdering providers. One section actually proposes that the terminally ill or otherwise "dispensable" antichoice zealots act in kamikaze fashion, sacrificing their lives in order to cause death or property damage. Then the book ends with a self-consciously chilling coda that begins: "The interview on the following pages is not for everyone." This in itself is a curious assertion because it seems to suggest that what has preceded the interview—talk of wreaking havoc in the name of free speech or stalking abortion providers and their staff members in the name of all-American, Constitution-sanctioned protest—in fact is for everyone.

The section supposedly is an interview with an Army of God representative who says that the goal of the group is to "drive the abortion industry underground with or without the sanction of government law." The supposed speaker goes on about the advantages of bombing clinics, then concludes in an increasingly "God-fearing," "Amerika"-loathing lather. Concluding that the removal of an abortion doctor's thumbs is as inadequate a remedy as passive resistance, the book advocates violent murder, conceding in the end that "execution is rarely gentle."

It was not so much as a response to the so-called Army of God manual as a recognition of the violence against my colleagues that led me to make a decision. First I assessed my choices. I could stop what I was doing, but that wasn't a valid option for me. Or I could do whatever I could to increase the odds that I would survive what proves to be a dangerous occupation. Driving a car can be dangerous, thus the seat belt, air bag, and other safety features. Riding a bike or horse can cause terrible head injuries, which causes me to wear a helmet whenever I engage in such activities. In other words, I realized that I do the best I can in virtually all activities to minimize the threats of physical injury. With that realization I determined that I would buy a bulletproof vest and wear it whenever I traveled to work and back.

Is the wearing of medieval-style armor the solution to dealing with barbaric threats? Was I only deluding myself in hoping to gain some feeling of security? Perhaps. But the decision had been made and now it was just a matter of finding out about the reality of wearing something ironically as cumbersome as the nuns' habits and Islamic chadors that had affected me so much during my formative years. It was time to go shopping.

14

Ducks, Flips, Panders

I suppose at the beginning of the bulletproof vest ordeal I never seriously thought I would be shot, much less killed. George Tiller, after all, had been injured by his assailant, but not so seriously as to prevent him from keeping up his work. He vowed at the time that he would return to work on the day following the shootings, even if it meant showing up in an ambulance. The purpose of the assault apparently had been to maim him—to go after his thumbs, in the metaphorical parlance of the Army of God manual. But no tendons had been severed, and he did return to work right away—a very brave decision, I might add.

Perhaps somewhat less bold was my initial thought about getting a bulletproof vest. I had no qualms about buying and wearing such a thing, but I said to a colleague that if procuring the item meant shopping at a gun store then the whole idea was out of the question. I'd been to precisely one gun-and-ammo shop before and it had just about given me a panic attack. The occasion presented itself when I needed to buy Cub Scout paraphernalia for one of my sons. Where we live, that meant going to a military-surplus-style store, which carries scout uniforms but also stocks all manner of guns and weaponry. While there I was appalled not only to see a young man stocking up on ammunition, but to overhear—as my son is my witness—a clerk ask him: "Will these bullets be for target practice or are they for killing people?"

So the notion of roaming into such a place for any reason gave me the creeps, to say nothing of the irony of having to venture into the realm of the gun culture in order to buy something to protect myself from guns. As it happened, such protective gear is sold not far from my clinic. It's available at a regular industrial-uniform store: uniforms for zoo workers and crosswalk guards; bulletproof gear for police and other human targets. The displays for the latter are instructive if not exactly reassuring, what with people posed in various combat stances exclaiming "Now you too can withstand gunfire!!!" Moreover, the women's movement seems to have prompted a form-fitted product line. Recognition by the commercial body-armor industry seems to be that the standard, flat-chested vest doesn't quite work for some people—female police officers, for example. Anyway, the clerk was explaining my options to me: how this caliber of fabric would withstand this or that impact and how that one would handle an incoming bullet. None of it was particularly what I wanted to hear, such was the dubious nature of this particular shopping trip. I would have given anything at the time to be back at my clinic, minding my own business and working without fear of assault. Then the clerk handed me a metal plate to be tucked in over the heart so that I could "take a hit and get right up and go after that assailant!" I said, disbelievingly: "Get right up and go after the assailant? What are you talking about? I'm not going after anybody. I'm going to be lying down desperately pretending to be dead." I learned I could withstand a stab to the chest with invincibility and could get shot up with anything less than an AK-47 assault rifle and still survive. There was a custom-sizing option in case I wanted something other than small, medium, or large. The armor ended up costing me

$600 plus tax. Moreover, I had to prove my need for such a high-tech make of this particular Kevlar garment, which is to say, being an abortion doctor is deemed an acceptable reason.

The practical reality is that wearing such a vest is uncomfortable and time-consuming. Usually I wear it under my outer garments but over shirts. To complain about how cumbersome or inconvenient the thing is misses the point—like objecting to car seat belts because they wrinkle your pants. If nothing else my sons have been able to look beyond the grim reminder of the abortion provider's vulnerability posed by the bulletproof vest. "You look really buff," one will say. "I'd be afraid to take you on looking like that." The other will tell me I look like a Mac truck. Obviously, neither look was exactly what I had in mind, but times change. The kids and my husband genuinely were glad that I'd done something positive about dealing with the threat of violence. They also were supportive when I told them that I'm just not willing to stop doing the work that I find so important, even though it means dragging around this second skin. Still, certain discussions have given me pause. On a walk one time my youngest asked what I'd do if I were wounded. "Would you keep working?" he wanted to know, and I told him I didn't know. I'd have to think about it. He said he hoped I'd keep working because "it would be really horrible to let those bad people win." My kids are obviously very prochoice children and aware of the value of the service I provide. The youngest has shown anxiety in the past, telling me "it's a drag" not knowing when he last sees me in the morning whether I'm going to be back that night. It would be good if that anxiety could disappear, but the repetition of violence is such that it never ends. First there's a killing in Pensacola, then a wounding in Wichita, and then a multiple murder in Pensacola, with its well-publicized trial. Then, just as that subsides, a doctor less than two hundred miles away in Vancouver, British Columbia, is gunned down in his own kitchen. Here's a man who was pulling himself along the kitchen floor in a pool of his own blood trying to warn his family members upstairs. His legs were saved and his brain is functioning fine. On the other hand, he's scarcely the whole person he was prior to the attack. His assault was a textbook stalking from the Army of God manual. Then a month later comes a kamikaze-style attack in Boston and another by the same man in Norfolk the next day.

It ought to occur to authorities to look at barriers that have been broken and patterns that have been established. First there was the taboo about actually assaulting abortion providers. Then came the barrier about hitting staff-workers of providers. Finally came the breaking point about shooting providers in their own homes. After the trail stretches from one coast to the other, with obvious signs that assaults have been prompted by the Army of God manual, which is in its sixth printing, from what we hear, there's no indication that authorities such as the FBI have any willingness to investigate any of this as a conspiracy. It's as though the political controversy that attends the general subject of abortion means that there's less of an imperative for police and the FBI to do anything about murderous assaults on abortion-clinic personnel.

Or, as exemplified by an incident of wild irony, authorities apply the law to the prochoice side. Such was the case in April 1995, as reported in regional newspapers, when a Washington man was charged under the Freedom of Access to Clinic Entrances Act. The latter was passed in 1994 as a means of prosecuting violent antichoice demonstrators. But in the April case the U.S. Justice Department applied the law to a prochoice man who said he had reacted to the Boston murders by getting drunk and placing threatening phone calls to antichoice offices. If this was the case, then of course the guilty party deserves his punishment. I don't condone such behavior. It would be the height of hypocrisy for me to do otherwise. On the other hand, one had to wonder why there would surface such a "man-bites-dog" slant on the application of the freedom-of-access law. It's fine to go after this alleged prochoice offender, but where was the equal zeal in going after an antichoice conspiracy? Perhaps

Eleanor Smeal best summed up the prochoice reaction. Speaking at the time as president of the Feminist Majority Foundation, she told reporters: "I'm puzzled. If this person is guilty, so be it, but there have been scores of threats against abortion providers and many instances of stalking. We cannot understand why they have not filed indictments in those cases." Speculation was that the Justice Department wanted to be viewed as neutral in its attempts to enforce the law. This was difficult to understand, however, when, at the time, only eight indictments had been made against antichoice activity.

One of the eight was against Paul Hill, the Florida man who has been convicted of the murder of Dr. John Bayard Britton and sentenced. Hill and other terrorists no doubt will become martyrs to the extreme antichoice fringe. I wish for Hill nothing less than a full lifetime in prison contemplating what he did to innocent people in Florida in July 1994. I consider it a moral tragedy that this murderer has been sentenced to death.

While I determined to write this book prior to Hill's crimes, I redoubled my commitment afterward. And, as remorseless as Paul Hill is, at least he committed his crimes in public and was easily apprehended. That's much more than can be said about the coward in Vancouver. Cowardice, of course, extends well beyond those who stealthily set off bombs and take shots at people. There was, in the aftermath of the Boston and Norfolk crimes, the unwillingness of many who either call themselves "prolife" or are antichoice to denounce these and other violent activities. Certain leaders of my own bygone Catholic church couldn't bring themselves to articulate an unequivocal denunciation of violence against abortion providers and clinics. Republican political hopefuls—and here are the true cowards of the issue—scurried about in the aftermath of the 1994 violence to "position" and "reposition" themselves on the subject of abortion. Some who are staunch in their opposition to choice such as Pat Buchanan and Phil Gramm hastened to strengthen such positions. Wafflers such as Bob Dole and Lamar Alexander sought to "clarify" their positions. The following *Time* magazine column of

April 17, 1995, written by Michael Kramer, demonstrates just how borderline comical it becomes when the subject of abortion rights provokes what the headline calls "Ducks, Flips and Panders": "Abortion is causing its normal fits, and the waffling prize on this issue goes to Lamar Alexander. As recently as last summer, Alexander was telling prospective supporters that his views were too nuanced for labels. 'That was okay for prochoicers like me,' says Mary Louise Smith, a leading Iowa GOP activist. 'I really don't understand his change.' Alexander today describes himself as prolife—with a tortured caveat about 'not wanting the government to subsidize, encourage or prohibit' abortion. When I asked if he would permit military personnel to get abortions at government hospitals, Alexander said: 'What are you talking about?' Since then, one Alexander aide has told me the candidate would restore the old prohibition; a second has said Alexander would continue Clinton's order; and a third has confessed that 'our position needs work.' "

Kramer's vignette would be hilarious if it were fiction. Instead, for most presidential candidates, past and present, the abortion subject prompts nothing but similar waffling, apologizing, and positioning. Prochoice Republican leaders, including Arlen Specter and Pete Wilson, who offered themselves early on as potential GOP presidential material, hoped during the earliest months of pre-primary jousting that abortion would become enough of a wedge issue to separate them from the antichoice candidates. The Specters and Wilsons (there are very few others among the Republican ranks) then seemed to view the issue less as a case of right versus wrong, and more as a vehicle for gaining the upper hand in a campaign. In this way, their posturing seemed more odious for its cynicism than Buchanan's and Gramm's did for the sinister implications of being so resolutely antichoice. Misguided as they are, at least the staunch antichoice politicians are up front about what they believe.

Why has abortion perennially been such a major campaign issue? Possibly because certain conservative politicians want it that way. They imagine luring blocs consisting of single-issue voters based on "positioning" themselves as antichoice. But this is sheer folly from a political perspective because polls all indicate that the overwhelming majority of Americans are prochoice. Moreover, most Americans are far less concerned about abortion than about economic issues: fair taxation, equal opportunity, job security, and the like. Politicians who play to such wedge issues as abortion and affirmative action only exacerbate the existing social problems.

On the other hand, during their more honest moments many candidates past and present, have conceded that they wish the abortion "issue" could be "taken off the table." That's what many of us thought had happened when the Supreme Court rendered its *Roe v. Wade* decision, but, as we see, the antichoice side has been unwilling to accept the idea that a woman's right to choose regarding matters affecting her own body is a right that precedes that of an embryo. If abortion really were, in campaign parlance, "taken off the table," then those of us who provide the procedure would be the happiest of all. We were happy with *Roe v. Wade* and have been pleased with every advance in birth-control procedures since then. When Mifepristone and similar pharmacological abortion remedies are perfected and made widely available, we'll be happier still. We'll be ecstatic when every woman on earth has the capability of deciding when and if she'll be pregnant, because we know that only such freedom can assure that millions of unwanted children aren't born and consigned to lives of misery by a world that seems to love the idea of pregnant women much more than the reality of nuisance children.

So it isn't with a sense of wanting confrontation that I write this book. Abortion providers aren't looking for quarrels and confrontations. We're only trying to do the work that we believe is of the utmost importance to women. I've always said that I do what I do because of an incredibly strong, solid, centered philosophic belief that my work is the right thing to do. It allows me to come home and look at my life after forty-seven years and say: "I've done something really positive for the world." Yet, being an abortion provider amounts to much less than a comfortable position to be in right now. First of all, it takes a lot of physical and emotional energy just to enter into a relationship with a woman who is dealing with a lot of intense pain and sorrow. Just that, with nothing else going on peripherally, requires a tremendous amount of psychological energy, to be able to say to each patient: "I understand your situation right now, and I honor you for what you've chosen to do. I support what you're doing. I'll take good care of you." Then we have the procedure itself to work through, after which I place the woman in the capable hands of my support staff and start with another client: This happens twenty times a day. That alone is plenty of expended energy for any normal human being. To add all the peripherals that exist right now is inhuman. I get home and I'm exhausted, and I'm more angry now than ever.

I'm more angered and disgusted by the antichoice movement than I ever was before. It appalls me that so many who voted in November of 1994 and who apparently support a conservative legislative agenda in my state and throughout the country can do so with such faint regard for women and children. So many recently elected officials are utter travesties for their lack of understanding of the needs of the poor, the sick, and the weak. The scant outcry in the wake of antiabortion terrorism is equally appalling. I feel as though I'm living under siege sometimes, as though this country had come under some mindless Sarajevo-like shelling, where acquiescence to wanton violence has become the norm. Courts in certain states have been hearing arguments in favor of overthrowing the federal law that protects the security of abortion clinics and the women who use them. Where's the moral outrage when this happens? Where's the outrage over an organized antichoice underground that is killing abortion providers? Granted, no forum here or anywhere has ever come up with a plan for protecting the vulnerable against terrorism. But where's the public denouncement? How can the archdiocese of major cities not speak out when a man walks into a Massachusetts clinic and murders innocent people? How dare anyone condone such killings? Even if the freedom to choose abortion were not legal, this failure to condemn would be unconscionable. But lost amid all the violence and indefensible silence is this: No matter what conservative religious officialdom and the rest of the antichoice forces choose to believe, the fact remains that abortion is not illegal in this country. Given the present composition and disposition of the U.S. Supreme Court, it isn't likely that *Roe* v. *Wade* will even be reconsidered anytime soon, much less overturned. If anything, the re-election of Clinton or the election of a moderate Republican no doubt would result in yet another prochoice Supreme Court appointment—perhaps more than one. The awareness of the futility of pursuing an antichoice agenda through the courts, then, is what has prompted the frustration that has led to antiabortion terrorism. Now it just remains to be seen how long law-enforcement agencies will be willing to allow such terrorism before doing something about it. If I had my way, the FBI would be pursuing aggressively the Army of God fanatics and like-minded antichoice people—some of them officials of the Catholic church itself (such as the Catholic priest David Trosch of Alabama, who has signed the Justifiable Homicide declaration*)—who advocate or commit violent acts against abortion clinics. I'll admit that the FBI and the Bureau of Alcohol, Tobacco, and Firearms have been very responsive to our calls. Realistically, though, what are they going to do? How are they going to protect the comings and goings of every abortion provider? How can they secure every abortion clinic against terrorism when outlaw organizations are encouraging kamikaze-style self-sacrifice? The truth is that there is no final, absolute protection against a determined terrorist. That means abortion providers have to live the remainder of their working lives at risk of being gunned down at any time—for offering a medical service that is perfectly legal and eminently necessary. It means there's nothing they can do about such threats. It

---

*According to the National Abortion Federation, Trosch has been reprimanded by his superior, Oscar Lipscomb, but has not as yet been defrocked for his advocacies.

means there's nothing their staffs or their families can do about it. It means that women seeking the safe havens of abortion clinics have no lasting guarantees that they'll be able to come and go without being assaulted or caught in a crossfire.

Americans, of course, have been saturated with tales of conspiracy. From the Kennedy assassination to the O.J. Simpson trial, many have supposed conspiracy theories to meet real or paranoid needs. Let it be recalled, then, that after the Paul Hill murders and the Vancouver shootings, one could have supposed that the pattern of terrorism, if projected onto a map, revealed a geographical diagonal. Then would the next major abortion-related act of terrorism happen in San Diego or Boston? And so, sure enough, a few weeks after the Vancouver incident came the horrifying attacks in Boston. Then, in the ensuing months, there were assaults in California. Was there a calculated pattern of terrorism? If so, who was calling the shots? Why doesn't the FBI know anything about it? And if it knows, why isn't it doing anything about these threats? Why the reticence of the U.S. attorney general's office, except in the case of one pro-choice man who may have made some unfortunate and indefensible phone calls? If these acts of terrorism were being leveled at other perfectly legal medical providers—orthodontists, say, or ophthalmologists—then wouldn't there be a public outcry about it? Or are we left with the conclusion that protecting of abortion providers is somehow less of a priority because abortion is more controversial than orthodontia or ophthalmology?

Where's the outcry from the press about abortion-clinic terrorism? After the Vancouver assault, newspapers printed the requisite hand-wringing editorials. But little has been written or spoken since then, despite the subsequent horrors in Boston. Maybe the media, which have to cover all of society's ills and so much violence, haven't yet grasped the genuine horror of antichoice terrorism. I find, that is, that I have to explain myself when I inform newspaper editors and TV reporters that I don't want my face photographed, and for good reason. After explaining to them what should be the obvious vulnerability of abortion providers, media people usually are apt to understand. After all, they grant such anonymity to all sorts of victims. I just wish they were as keen on reporting about the violent antichoice underground as they are about the crimes themselves, to say nothing of the victims of the crimes. For information about abortion-clinic terrorism I find I have to depend on my colleagues because the press doesn't follow up on the stories. That's how I know about this poor man in Vancouver dragging himself across a bloody floor trying desperately to call an emergency phone number while straining to keep his wife and son out of harm's way. Why are the media reluctant to pursue stories about antichoice terrorism? Is it because abortion is controversial? Because it involves women? Because it involves women deemed to have done something wrong? Because there's a risk of alienating a segment of the readership or viewing audience? Perhaps the crux of society's reticence about abortion-clinic terrorism stems from a vague perception even among enlightened people that abortion involves something not quite right.

But then society is reticent on all sorts of issues involving women. Family abandonment by fathers is said by both liberals and conservatives to be a major cause of poverty and related social problems in this country. But seldom is there heard a united voice condemning deadbeat fathers. Is it because the father's role in causing unwanted pregnancy is seen as less culpable in leading to negative social consequences? Do we really believe that pregnancy is basically the woman's responsibility or the woman's fault?

Of course there are heroic fathers who take responsibility for their roles in making and nurturing children. We see responsible fathers every week at our clinic. They accompany their partners, they grieve with them, they go home with them, and they are there, presumably, when the time comes to plan responsibly for families. They're the fathers who understand the equal role they play in child-rearing and who are there for their partners and their kids, with no silly qualms about such notions as delineating domestic duties in terms of the sex-stereotyped dictates and expectations of the past. These are among the most fulfilled, self-actualized men I know. They are men who understand that much of what is wrong in the world stems from senseless sexual animosity caused by generations—centuries, in some cultures—of male domination. They are strong, confident, and secure enough about themselves to know that feminist women don't carry with them some diabolical male-domination agenda. Any reasonable person would have long since come to terms with the ideas of equality and freedom and would have agreed with Abraham Lincoln's assertion that when some are not free, then no one is truly free. No self-respecting feminist woman would dominate men any more than she would want to be dominated by a male hierarchy.

But for all its nuances and subtleties male domination persists. In an almost naive way I have the sense that if I could just sit down, one-on-one, with people and explain my beliefs, then I could convince them that what I'm doing is right. I know it can't happen in a debate format, because abortion obviously doesn't lend itself to the kind of "Crossfire" confrontations that quickly degenerate into accusations and shouting matches. In fact, not much can be resolved about abortion until the antichoice side concedes that the issue is not about baby-killing but about the sovereign right of a human being to make the decisions that affect her own body.

What I'm left with is a near dilemma when considering my career options. In order to assure greater personal safety, I can either quit performing abortions, which I find utterly unacceptable, or I can take every reasonable measure possible to see that my safety and the safety of my coworkers and family members is secure. Should abortion providers have to be resigned to such a dilemma? Of course we shouldn't. But until society finds better ways to deal with the sexual inequality that leads to vulnerability of abortion providers and their patients, the dilemma will remain. And fortunately, as we'll see, the possibility of affecting the end of unwanted pregnancies with pills instead of surgical procedures means we may be at the threshold of the best way yet to thwart the antichoice groups.

Part Three

Still Waiting

15

The Abortion Pill

I've been working toward the goal of testing Mifepristone since 1989. I had read about the drug, known popularly as RU 486, from 1988 and was aware when we traveled to France that physicians there were experimenting with what came to be known as "the French abortion pill." In 1989, while in France, I went to Paris to observe the drug being applied, and that year I also attended a world conference in London on the subject. Eleanor Smeal, past president of the National Organization for Women, also attended that conference and we've kept in touch. Since then I've attended the two important American conferences about Mifepristone, the most recent in Washington, D.C.

This is essentially how the drug works. Mifepristone, which is introduced into a pregnant woman's system as a pill, is an antiprogesterone drug. The pregnant woman needs the hormone progesterone to keep the walls of the uterus intact and give the conceptus a good place to grow during the process of vascularization (in which the conceptus attaches to the uterine wall and draws nourishment from the blood vessels there). Mifepristone is an antagonist that blocks the ability of progesterone to act on its receptor cells, which happen to be abundant in the uterus. By introducing Mifepristone, the cells in the uterus are unable to do all that is necessary to keep the pregnancy viable. The blood vessels break down and withdraw; the conceptus is separated from the uterine wall; the cervix softens; the uterine muscles contract; and, after the second dose of drugs this time using Misoprostol, a prostaglandin (a drug which causes contraction of the uterine muscles), the conceptus is expelled very strongly. This is the way the drug is supposed to work. The fact that it isn't 100 percent effective is noted in Appendix E.

This background placed me at the American forefront of awareness about Mifepristone. I have spoken about it publicly whenever possible and I also address it privately whenever the subject comes up. For this reason, my clinic has been an obvious candidate for testing in the United States, an opportunity which finally happened in 1994. That was when the World Population Council finally secured permission from the Food and Drug Administration to test the abortion pill. I had attended a preliminary meeting in New York during the summer of 1993, when the Population Council convened abortion providers who had expressed an interest in offering test sites for Mifepristone. My interest in becoming a testing agent stemmed from my understanding of the subject and because my abortion clinic had led the way with Depoprovera and Norplant.

The population council's mission at the outset was to see whether Mifepristone could pass several tests. Could the clinics, for example, complete the testing in a nonhostile environment? Would the drug be administered safely without adverse physical side effects? Would American women embrace this nonsurgical abortion method with an approval level similar to that of French women?

But there obviously is much more to Mifepristone than safety, effectiveness, and acceptance. If women can go to any physician and be given a drug to end unwanted pregnancies, then the antichoice side can no longer single out abortion clinics or surgical-abortion providers as targets. The antichoice advocates are only too aware of this. It's a situation reminiscent of what happened when the oppressed masses of the Soviet Union and its Eastern Bloc countries overthrew totalitarianism during the late 1980s. For decades tyrants had been able to keep populations in check with the threat of terrorism. But once the masses had been exposed to democracy—however limited its scope—there was no containing these oppressed people. No longer could threats of terror be universally applied, and with that realization despots lost control of their military regimes and ultimately lost control of the people. Likewise, in theory, with a universally available abortion pill, antichoice terrorists could no longer intimidate clinics and patients because the availability of abortion would have been much more universally dispersed. In short, no one who would take the trouble to observe comings and goings could have any idea what a woman was doing when she went to her family physician for Mifepristone treatment. She would leave looking just as she did when she arrived, only she'd have three pills in her system and two more in her purse to be taken during the next week. Then she'd return after two weeks for a follow-up examination and that would be that.

If acceptance of the Mifepristone treatment proceeds as I anticipate, the number of surgical abortions in the United States will be reduced by 30 to 40 percent within fifteen years. Our methods as providers will include overlapping options. During the first few weeks of pregnancy women will be able to abort using drugs. Thereafter, the surgical method will be available along with the drug method. After eight weeks from the previous menstrual period we'll be able to offer strictly surgical abortions, as is now the case. Each method will overlap the other, with the patient being able to help decide the treatment in virtually all early pregnancies.

What is the advantage of Mifepristone? There are several, not the least of which is psychological. Women invariably believe the pill method to be more of a "natural" way to abort (see appendices). On the other hand, women remain well aware that any abortion procedure is serious. Yes, we offer safe, nearly painless surgical-abortion procedures. Yes, we honor the women who make this choice. And yet, having said all this, and having undergone an abortion myself, I can say in all honesty that the experience is a sobering one. The one major difference we noticed during the first days of offering Mifepristone was that women coming in for a nonsurgical abortion procedure showed much less shame or guilt, much more pride than women being treated surgically. This could have to do with a number of factors, not the least of which is the realization that they wouldn't be having to submit to an intrusive surgical procedure. We speculated that perhaps patients would see the abortion pill as a "cleaner" procedure than surgical abortion, although in truth the drug carries side effects such as cramping and bleeding. But there's no public spectacle involved with Mifepristone, even though many on the antichoice side have referred to the drug as "human insecticide." In fact, it's a safe procedure. I found it fascinating during our early experimentation that patients viewed Mifepristone as a much more "natural" method of abortion. Taking a pill was deemed more "natural" than a surgical procedure. Putting a pill into your system meant that the uterus would be given cause to do the entire abortion procedure on its own, with no aid from a physician. That's what "natural" apparently had come to mean. Very possibly what the women also meant was that it is a much more private means of achieving the same end.

Does Mifepristone, then, blunt the swords of the antichoice forces once and for all? Not necessarily. By having like-minded people elected to office, the antichoice sentiment no doubt will be reflected in a regulatory frenzy the like of which we've never seen before. Imposing more bureaucracy on abortion providers, of course, is hypocritical in an environment of government nonintervention. Opposed to maintaining clean-water standards or land-use regulations, these same politicians are quick to intervene where abortion is concerned, with enforced waiting periods for minors of twenty-four to forty-eight hours. Such a mindset is against "interfering with privacy" if it means helping poor women or homeless children who are already born, but interfering in the case of embryos is different. Such interference defines the antichoice moral raison d'être and focuses their crusade. Besides, it's much easier to harp about the unborn. Why work to help existing children when embryos require no assistance other than that rendered by incessant protesting, posturing, and terrorism? Would the antichoice people ever devote any effort to helping poor women? No, because the ultimate desire of most of the antichoice persuasion is the total subjugation of women, a totally male-dominated, "patriarchal" society.

On the other hand, maybe the next election will swing the other way. Perhaps Americans who saw the so-called fairness of the "Contract with America" for what it really was—a con job on the poor and middle classes for the benefit of the wealthy, mainly white-male establishment—will vote for candidates who will try to solve social problems rather than exacerbate existing ones.

Fortunately there isn't going to be any public vote on the subject of drug-induced abortions. David Kessler, the progressive head of the Food and Drug Administration (FDA), is prochoice and in favor of Mifepristone treatment. What remains prior to the drug being cleared for use is the analysis of information my clinic and several others have been gathering since the fall of 1994. The results of the analysis will be based on 2,000 doses of Mifepristone, distributed equally among the testing clinics.

With the U.S. experiment we wanted to go beyond the mere gauging of acceptance of the process. We assumed there would be great acceptance of Mifepristone, even though it also seemed obvious that a lot of women would need to be advised that the treatment is somewhat more involved than merely swallowing a couple of pills at prescribed intervals. We needed to go beyond qualitative observations and get into more quantitative analysis. Specifically, we wanted to test results with extensions of the period of use. In France, the procedure is never used after forty-nine days of pregnancy (that's forty-nine days from the most recent menstrual period). In our study we had a second group using the procedure from fifty to fifty-six days and a third from fifty-seven to sixty-three days, nine weeks in the latter instance. We were able to make all the dating extremely precise with the use of ultrasound.

My earliest hypothesis underestimated demand for Mifepristone treatment. There was such a flurry of media publicity during the first few weeks of the experiment that I assumed it was accounting for the inordinate interest in the procedure. After all, we had done no advertising. We originally had a month-long waiting list, after which I figured interest would wane somewhat. But after six months, such was the level of interest that we found we still weren't having to do any recruiting. Some of the women who selected the procedure had undergone previous surgical abortions. But whether they had or not, all the women said they chose the Mifepristone procedure because it seemed less intrusive than the surgical method. Another common trait among the Mifepristone recipients was their dedication to the testing itself. On their written forms and in interviews these women made it very clear that they wanted to be part of this because they want this treatment to be available for all women, present and future. That, of course, demonstrates a solidarity among women that is extremely gratifying.

It's especially gratifying given that the test-case women had to be heavily involved in paper work and other procedures in order to help document the study. For them there was much more to the process than just coming in, taking a pill, and going home. They had to answer to a strict set of criteria that included age (they had to be eighteen or older) and concurrent medical problems. Asthma sufferers, for example, were not allowed to participate because prostaglandins can affect asthmatics adversely. If a potential candidate smoked it had to be less than half a pack per day. They couldn't be afflicted with ovarian cancer or carry an active infection in the uterus or fallopian tubes. We also took into consideration past reproductive problems. Of course, study subjects had to have a documented intrauterine (not ectopic) pregnancy. After fulfilling all the test criteria, the women also had to agree to stay in town for a few weeks. They had to live within a couple hours' drive of the clinic in case there were problems. They also had to commit to spending three or four hours in the clinic filling out forms and answering questions during the initial visit and two return trips.

My staff and I initially underestimated the level of privacy women would want during their subsequent visits. I suppose we were unaware at the beginning of the study that women might not want to sit in the waiting room having mild cramps for a few hours and taking turns going to the bathroom while watching movies on television. We soon determined that they invariably would want to have their own private space. It was little wonder since the women would be experiencing discomfort and bleeding the first half hour after taking the Misoprostol pill. Many of the women expressed surprise that there would be as much bleeding as there was: much more than with a menstrual period.

Some of the women briefly remarked on the passing of the pregnancy, saying, "Oh, look, everybody, it's happening." There seemed to be a much more positive atmosphere surrounding the study than we might have normally observed during surgical procedures. They knew they were playing a vital part in proving that this procedure worked, and they were extremely proud to have been involved. Granted, some women were upset at having to see the embryo pass with the pregnancy tissue. This is understandable. Contrary to what some critics would have us believe, no woman blithely makes the decision to end an unwanted pregnancy. Even though these patients realize that making a decision to have an abortion is the right thing for them under the circumstances, having made the decision doesn't necessarily mitigate their feelings during and after the procedure.

Generally, however, the enthusiasm for the experiment was positive from start to finish, as we'll see in subsequent chapters and in the appendices featuring interviews with Mifepristone test-case women. Those who had doubts early on about the procedure either were assuaged or dissuaded after initial conversations over the phone. Those who chose to proceed were required to read the consent form and sign it before any further action was taken. They would learn that there might be a lot of bleeding and that surgery might be required to stop it. Some would think again about the prospect of having to come to the clinic three times and they'd decide that, no, they didn't want to do it after all. But it wasn't as though being dissuaded about Mifepristone made any women change their minds about abortion in general. They were given the same surgical options and were told they could have a surgical abortion either that day or within the ensuing few days. Assuming the women still wanted the Mifepristone, the next major point of concern would occur if the ultrasound indicated they were too far along for the pill procedure. No doubt there were women genuinely committed to being in the study who might have wanted us to fudge our estimated pregnancy dates, but they realized that doing so would have jeopardized the entire scientific experiment. Besides, doing so might have guaranteed those women a higher failure rate and a greater risk of bleeding. We discerned, in fact, a greater failure rate and more bleeding in women in groups two and three as opposed to the women whose pregnancies hadn't progressed beyond forty-nine days.

When I say "failure" that meant one of two things, the least likely being that the pregnancy hadn't been aborted. That was extremely rare. The greater risk was that, while the pregnancy no longer was viable, the conceptus hadn't yet been completely expelled from the uterus. In the rare case of a pregnancy that was still ongoing after drug treatment we strongly recommended surgical abortion. The Mifepristone and Misoprostol would adversely affect the pregnancy. Of course we couldn't and wouldn't force any women to abort pregnancies that remained ongoing after Mifepristone treatment. But we certainly would always try our hardest to persuade them about the risks to the fetus.

What did women tell us? Of the first 150 we treated with Mifepristone, only two told us afterward that they would never recommend the procedure to a friend and would never consider going through it again. This is compared with the vast majority of women who reported that it was difficult between days one and three knowing that they'd taken the first pill and had started a process that was virtually irreversible. They'd started something that was going on in their bodies and they realized they had a lot longer to live with their decisions than they would have had they opted for the surgical procedure. Some of these women complained about bleeding or nausea or cramping. Yet, to a woman, they also said that they would do it again, they would recommend it to other women, and it was much more natural this way. Even those women who said they might not want to use the procedure again insisted that they could easily see how the treatment might be right for other women. The solidarity about a woman's right to choose was unanimous. The recurring remark about how relatively "natural" the procedure seemed to be was voiced regardless of what we in the medical profession may believe about what constitutes a "natural" bodily function. The inference I drew was that it tends to be tremendously empowering for women to be able to make the decision to swallow the medication and then let their own bodies do the work. Many were quite disappointed if later we had to perform a surgical rescue to empty the uterus in those instances in which the medication didn't make the abortion happen on its own, or "naturally."

Others found that there was a bonus of sorts when they arrived the day of the procedure. Test subjects were given the drug treatment at no charge. I doubt whether it would have been the deciding factor for any of the women—even the least financially able (and some of the women who contacted us were unable to afford birth-control pills, much less abortions). Then again, $300 is no small matter, and that's what many of the women in the test group saved by taking part in the study. They also gained greatly with the awareness that they were pioneers in what could prove to be one of the major empowering innovations in modern reproductive medicine for American women.

16

Toward Greater Enlightenment

Women who were interested in being part of the Mifepristone study were asked over the phone to bring $300 with them when they came in for their initial appointment. That way, we explained, if for some reason they didn't meet the criteria for the study they would still be able to have a surgical abortion. We were extremely careful during the early stages of the testing to say as little as possible about the fact that the test women would receive the Mifepristone free of charge. If the procedure became inordinately appealing merely for the cost factor, then the study in effect could be seen as enticing the poorest women to take part. This says plenty about the dreadful state of birth control in America. One wonders how many women in the United States would have had far less burdensome lives if only, at a critical juncture, they could have afforded to follow through on their desire to end unwanted pregnancies. Making the decision should have nothing to do with a woman's socioeconomic status. The poorest and least educated of women will, when faced with an unwanted pregnancy, make precisely the same decision as that of a Harvard-educated woman with money in her bank account. The tragedy, then, is that society could deny access to abortion based solely on a woman's ability to pay for the procedure. I believe the government should pay for abortions for poor women just like it pays for prenatal care and hysterectomies for poor women—because it's part of legal, medically accepted reproductive health-care.

Nevertheless, in order to try to maintain the integrity of the experiment during the early going, we deliberately avoided telling women that the procedure was free until after they'd been accepted for the study. This wasn't easy. Women would call and ask about cost and we would waffle, saying: "Well, we'd like you to bring the $300 and we'll run through the criteria and we don't want anybody's decision to be based on cost." But as the word got around, women would call and tell us they'd heard the procedure was free. Needless to say, we couldn't deny it, so the test women in effect saved the $300 they normally would have paid for surgical procedures.

The savings could be considered a way of saying "thanks" to the test-case women. If so, it seems a small amount to pay for pioneering research. While I obviously consider such research heroic, there have been some even from prochoice circles who have posed the peculiar argument that a more accessible form of abortion somehow could result in women minimizing the entire notion of pregnancy. Such was the odd subtext of a February 1995 article in the medical journal *Hippocrates* in which the author, in effect, suggested that the availability of an abortion pill made the whole notion of abortion almost too easy for women. (A similar suspicion is raised by a woman whose Mifepristone experience is recounted in Appendix D.) The author, Louise Levathes, wrote that "because a woman administers the drug to herself, it is a much more deliberate and conscious experience, and is more likely to force a woman to confront her true feelings about her pregnancy and the moral dilemma of abortion."*

_____

*See Louise Levathes, "It's Reputed to Be an Easy One-Step Abortion Pill," *Hippocrates* (February 1995).

I discussed the article with my executive director, who drew the same inference from the piece. It was the same old reasoning: Women have done something terrible by becoming pregnant and they should have to suffer in dealing with it, though, as we've discussed, the miscarriage-like process is somewhat more involved than merely taking pills and getting on with one's life. The argument wasn't much different in spirit from the regulatory hoop-jumping my clinic and others have had to perform or from the legislative restrictions some states have imposed or tried to impose. In fact, it wasn't different from the essence of the antichoice belief that women should be subjugated and that their bodies are the property of the state. Pregnancy, the argument goes, needs to be associated directly with shame: Shame on any woman who might desire to relieve herself of an unwanted pregnancy.

It was, then, an utterly unenlightened way to greet a promising study that test-case women were willingly embracing. They would arrive at our clinic one of the two days during the week we had set aside for the study. We had appointed a particular staff woman to be the "Mifepristone person" for each day. That way the pregnant women only had to deal with one main contact person, who would take them through the consent form and explain to them the rather considerable array of paper work. Then the staff member would go over the general criteria for the study. If a pregnant woman fit the criteria and agreed to the three visits, then she would be sent to the nurse-practitioner who would perform a pelvic exam and an ultrasound analysis. That would reveal whether the woman's pregnancy ranged anywhere from a discernible sac to our sixty-three-day cutoff point. If so, she would be sent back to the appointed Mifepristone staff member, who would take a very thorough medical history, draw blood specimens, and explain the drug treatment procedure. Then the patient would be sent back to the nurse-practitioner for a complete physical exam. If the woman was then accepted as a candidate she would be given the Mifepristone pill, which she would swallow at the clinic following the study protocol and under my direction. The administering of the pill itself was simply to hand it to the woman in a paper cup, have her swallow it with some water, and have her remain in the clinic for fifteen minutes to be sure she didn't vomit the medication. Normally this wouldn't happen. But one woman, sure enough, was in a hurry and left the clinic immediately after swallowing the medication. Fifteen minutes later she vomited in her car and had to turn around, come back, calm down, have a little cola and soda cracker, and try again. This time she managed to keep it down. Another woman ended up in the emergency room after repeated vomiting, but not because of the Mifepristone. She managed to keep the pill down, but she'd always had a lot of vomiting with her pregnancies and this one was no exception. She vomited into the night, then went to an emergency room, where she was hooked up to IVs. The next day she staggered into our office and we started more IVs to deal with the dehydration from the vomiting. She wanted a surgical procedure right away. We could certainly perform the abortion, but I had to make her aware that since she had already started the drug treatment, her vomiting might not subside after the surgical procedure. The drug would have to wear off. She eventually decided to stick with the drug treatment, and as soon as she passed the tissue she started feeling better. Part of her recovery was psychological, but part was physiological, too, because the pregnancy hormone levels which cause nausea begin to drop very rapidly with the passage of the conceptus.

Nausea was a problem for some women. Others experienced cramping. About 40 percent started having cramps within twelve hours of taking the first pills. Fewer than I expected started bleeding after the Mifepristone was administered. In fact, there was a minimum of bleeding between days one and three. Other than that, the test subjects said they weren't aware of anything going on, aside from the fact that they had taken the medicine.

On day three they would come into the clinic and be asked whether they felt they'd passed the tissue. If they thought they had, then either the nurse-practitioner or I would look with ultrasound. If the uterus proved to be empty, the woman wouldn't receive the next dose of medication. That happened just once in the case of a very early pregnancy. If the woman didn't think she had passed the tissue and hadn't had any bleeding, then she was given the Misoprostol. Usually within a half hour she would begin to get chills, cramps, bleeding, or any combination of the three. About half of the women would continue to experience these symptoms for three to four hours while waiting at the clinic. Another third to half wouldn't start experiencing heavy cramping or bleeding for a few hours. Some of these women needed to stay an extra hour if there was continued heavy bleeding, but we didn't have to keep anyone more than an additional hour. A few women would experience very minimal cramping and/or bleeding. They (as did the other women) received ultrasound before leaving. This was to see whether there was an ongoing pregnancy. If so, we told them that obviously they would be doing most of their cramping and bleeding at home (as was the case with two of the women interviewed in the appendices). They would end up passing the embryo at home, and they indicated they were emotionally prepared for that. Some would continue bleeding off and on for up to six weeks. A problem with adverse reactions, such as continued bleeding, has been that we've been unable to predict when or in which types of situations these reactions take place. None of my patients has bled in sufficient volume to require a blood transfusion, but one woman who lives within an hour of the clinic got home on a Friday and within two hours had her husband call from home to tell us she was bleeding heavily. We suggested that she come back immediately, but on the way the husband took her to an emergency room because she was starting to faint. That was an appropriate response to an adverse event. But it indicates that there will be difficult on-call situations in the future, because we know a certain number of women are going to require surgery for heavy bleeding. The problem is that we can't predict which women will need surgery or when they'll need it. We've had a case in which the patient required surgery for her bleeding six weeks after the treatment.

I've tempered my enthusiasm for using the Mifepristone procedure beyond forty-nine days. When I teach about the procedure, I'm quick to inform people about this qualified enthusiasm. I also point out that abortion providers are going to have to be willing to be available for surgery, as are emergency rooms and women's physicians. There will be a definite percentage of women who will require follow-up surgery, and the fact remains that it's less expensive for them to come into clinics such as ours for the surgical procedure than to go to hospitals. I plan to advocate using the drug and telling physicians that it's a safe procedure, but I also will tell them that they need to be aware of the possible surgical consequences. Now it could also be that we'll find other methods that will mitigate heavy bleeding. Possibly we'll change the dosage of the prostaglandins or place the medication in the vagina rather than sending it in pill form through the gastrointestinal system. Maybe that will result in such a lowering of the rate of incomplete abortions that it will affect the need for subsequent surgery.

All of this must wait until the study is finished and the FDA has given its approval to use Mifepristone. The FDA said prior to our experimentation that it would accept the findings of European testing. This was extremely unusual, but it was very gratifying to those who anticipate the value of Mifepristone treatment. It also posed yet another juxtaposition of congressional attitudes. On the one hand, conservative members of Congress are all for the FDA loosening restrictions on medications coming in from other countries, thereby reducing the time it takes to get vitally needed treatments on the market. However, many of these same people are opposed to allowing Mifepristone. Here again, were it not for the strong support from President Clinton and David Kessler, it's anybody's guess as to where we'd be with getting Mifepristone certified for use in this country. As it is, use of the drug still awaits finding an American manufacturer. The European manufacturer has cited insurance concerns in its refusal to make the drug available in the United States. The manufacturer did, however, donate the patent to the World Population

Council, so we know how to make the drug. What awaits us after the test results have been analyzed is for the FDA to approve the methodology of some prospective domestic manufacturer. As of mid-1995 the Population Council hadn't indicated whether a manufacturer had stepped forward. It was my assumption, though, that there wouldn't have been an expensive study undertaken had the council not received indications that manufacturers were interested. When will we see Mifepristone available for American women? My guess is that it will be late 1997 at the earliest. It could in fact be three years after that, depending on political factors. The election in 1996 of a strongly antichoice president could cause problems for a prospective manufacturer even if the FDA has approved Mifepristone by then. Pressure from the antichoice side is certain to come to bear should, say, Bob Dole or Phil Gramm be elected president. Any antichoice leader could delay Mifepristone indefinitely.

As much as I look forward to the availability of medication-induced abortions, I have some very definite personal opinions about the use of Mifepristone. Speaking for myself, then, if I were carrying anything less than a ten-millimeter-in-diameter sac (which would be the equivalent of a pregnancy of two and a half weeks, or four weeks since the most recent menstrual period), then I would choose the Mifepristone treatment. But I would do so only because of the increased possibility of missing such a small sac during a surgical abortion. For any pregnancy beyond that I would choose a five-minute surgical procedure without question. I'd want to take my pain medication, have my friends around, and just get it over with quickly. My view of what constitutes "natural" may very well differ from that of other women. My concern would be to end the pregnancy, and I still believe that a quick, safe surgical abortion is the easiest way to do it. I should stress that there is a real possibility of missing a sac of nine millimeters or less. My miss rate at ten millimeters or greater is nearly zero. Before ultrasound I was inclined to tell women who were just two-weeks pregnant to wait two to four weeks and come back and see me before having the surgical procedure. But with

ultrasound I can get a better indication of all the pertinent size factors. For example, at two-weeks pregnant the uterus is barely larger
than the smallest instruments we use. An early pregnancy also
means the cervix is barely softened. This isn't to say that I won't or
don't do procedures at such an early stage. It's just that I've set ten
millimeters as a minimum standard for being able to guarantee a virtually nonexistent failure rate.

The primary issue is the woman's well-being. Little has been
made of the fact that clinics such as mine have been instrumental in
saving the lives of women by terminating pregnancies. We have, for
example, made enormous progress in saving women from molar and
ectopic pregnancies. This has a lot to do with the fact that women
are coming to see us much earlier in their pregnancies. Let's say a
woman has an ectopic pregnancy, which means that the embryo is
growing somewhere other than in the uterus. We've found that we
can treat this with the drug Methotrexate and in so doing prevent
the growth from literally rupturing the side of the woman's uterus or
her fallopian tube. We can, then, save the woman's uterus so that she
can choose to become pregnant again. Moreover, our intervention
can prevent other serious consequences such as severe bleeding and,
ultimately, death. A molar pregnancy is one in which an abnor-
mally growing tumor that makes something similar to a pregnancy
sac produces pregnancy hormones but never results in an embryo.
We think it has to do with an abnormal sperm. On occasion these
molar pregnancies can become cancerous, because the growing tissue is made up of erratic cells. With ultrasound we can discern
whether such a condition exists and deal with it both with medication and by emptying the uterus. In so doing, we can save the
woman's uterus and save her life.

We don't yet know what percent of American women will be
choosing medication abortions instead of surgical procedures. In
France about 40 percent of women who are eligible select the drug
procedure. Here I anticipate an initial flurry of interest when the
drug becomes available. Women will read that it's here, it's ready, it's

on the shelf. We'll respond by conducting educational seminars. During the first two years there will be widespread use of Mifepristone. By then, I believe physicians will become more concerned about being called in the middle of the night to perform follow-up surgery for women who are bleeding heavily. Eventually the use of Mifepristone should moderate, perhaps to about the same percentage level as France.

Mifepristone, because of its attention in the media, can help generate widespread discussion among women, pregnant or otherwise. One of the great advantages of the entire Mifepristone study is that it has opened up discussion about abortion in general. I have mentioned in previous chapters that the subject of surgical abortion normally doesn't make it into dinner-party conversation. Reluctance to talk about the abortion in itself helps perpetuate the idea that it's a forbidden topic. But the Mifepristone study has prompted just the opposite response, and not only among women. It's much more socially acceptable in mixed gatherings to talk about an abortion pill than it ever was to ask such a thing as: "Does anybody know where I can find a good abortion clinic?" Talking about such a thing as an abortion pill doesn't seem to put one as much at risk as seeming to be seeking an abortion. Women have been much less reticent about discussing among themselves the efficacy of medication versus surgical procedures. This could be seen as surprising in the sense that there wasn't much public discussion about the Mifepristone testing after the initial wave that followed the announced FDA study sites in fall 1994. After November 1994 we scarcely heard anything about the subject from the popular media.

Americans, of course, could benefit greatly from a more frank and open public discourse about reproductive matters in general. We would, for example, prevent the demand for untold numbers of abortions if only we were to open up talk about so-called morning-after contraception. But, as we'll see in the next chapter, there is an almost ridiculous secret consensus in this country that says: The less we know about sexual matters, the less likely we'll be to suffer any bad consequences from sex. It is, here again, a kind of ostrich mentality: If we stick our heads in the sand, then everything bad will cease to exist. Perhaps it would be somewhat comforting for us to know that a growing number of Americans have concluded that sex education is itself the best tool we have for dealing with adverse consequences from sexual behavior. But even a relatively enlightened administration was capable of expelling then Surgeon General Joycelyn Elders because she dared to state what should be obvious to anyone who has thought seriously about sex. Right-wing America felt threatened when Elders asserted that the availability of condoms would both curb unwanted teen pregnancies and help fight the spread of sexually transmitted disease. But when she also mentioned that school children should be taught about masturbation—as they should, along with all other sexual matters—it was as though she'd advocated sexual abuse rather than enlightenment.

Where were the enlightened physicians and public-health authorities when Elders needed them to come to her defense? They were hard to find, and perhaps this was understandable in view of how utterly lacking in information many of my colleagues are when it comes to sex-related information. As we'll see, many women looking for a way to end an unwanted pregnancy already, in effect, could find such a remedy in the de facto abortion pills in the drawers of their nightstands. And a lot of women would be aware of what these pills can do for them if only their physicians knew enough to tell them about it in the first place.

17

The Morning-After Solution

What would it require to make significant changes in American attitudes about sex and reproduction? It would take nothing less than a complete transformation of American social mores about sexuality, a metamorphosis not likely to be witnessed any time soon. In the meantime, maybe we can move away from the mindset that, if you're informed about something—if you take the time to be as knowledgeable as you can be about sex and reproduction—then it necessarily follows that you're going to do something irresponsible. The corollary, as mentioned in the previous chapter, is that being uninformed about sex is to assure that there won't be any sexual behavior and therefore there won't be any adverse consequences. This is the assumption of the antichoice crowd and of anyone who believes ignorance about sex is beneficial. I have yet to see a lack of information about sex be a deterrent to sexual activity. On the contrary, teen pregnancies are far more likely to result from lack of information, and pregnant teenagers (and the young men who impregnate them) are among the least informed members of society.

This leads to an equally bewildering situation when considering that even sex partners who potentially have an unwanted pregnancy could—if only they knew how—easily obtain the results of an abortion but without surgery. They could use what has been called "morning-after" birth control. Such a method is believed by many to be a matter of conjecture or possibility or science fiction. But it is already available. *However, because of possible harmful side effects, women must consult their physician before using this method.* It simply involves taking two regular-dose birth-control pills (or four low-dose pills) within seventy-two hours of conception and two more regular pills (or four more low-dose) twelve hours later. If everyone knew about this method, I'm convinced there would be considerably fewer unwanted pregnancies and, accordingly, fewer surgical abortions.

Actually this method ought to be considered emergency contraception. It's not a recommendable method to use month after month, and there are definite risks. One is that taking an extra birth-control pill can cause vomiting, and if this happens before the medication gets into the system then the woman needs to repeat the procedure—always under the advice and care of a physician. But let's look at situations in which many of us have found ourselves. What if the condom breaks during intercourse? What if, in the heat of passion, no condom is used? All the woman needs to do in such a case is take the extra birth-control pills. The method is 97 percent effective in preventing the implantation of a fertilized egg.* In some women it even disrupts the fertilization process. It's a method that is almost ridiculously easy. By rights it ought to be one of the first facts about sexuality learned by every adolescent in the world.

How many know about emergency birth control? A *New York Times* story that focused on a group spreading the word about the method leads me to believe that the number could be relatively encouraging. Perhaps as much as 20 percent of the population that

---

*Robert A. Hatcher et al., *Contraceptive Technology*, 16th rev. ed. (New York: Irvington Publishing, 1994), p. 415.

could benefit from knowing about the method already is aware of it. On the other hand, maybe this is no great cause for celebration. Indeed, it is the general lack of information about emergency birth control that puzzles me. In my most skeptical of moments it occurs to me that it amounts to a deliberate suppression of information by a patriarchy whose members don't want women to know about the method. On the other hand, it's safe to say that much of the same white-male, older patriarchy also doesn't have a clue about such a thing as emergency birth control, and consequently couldn't possibly keep the information from being circulated. Cluelessness seems to be pervasive in some corners of the patriarchy.

In any case, let's grant many Americans the benefit of the doubt. Let's assume that they know about sex, pregnancy, condoms, and AIDS. Then why is it that this one critical bit of information is left out of the mix of facts? Let's pose the question differently. Let's say that 100 percent of American school children, as part of their general sex education, were taught that they could prevent an unwanted pregnancy after intercourse with birth-control pills. What would the result be? I'm absolutely convinced it would result in at least 50 percent fewer unwanted pregnancies in this country. Just imagine how that would translate as far as the general well-being in this country, especially for women and families already burdened beyond their means. Think of what it would mean as far as reducing the number of unwanted teen pregnancies.

What are the harmful side effects that society could cite? One is that the woman might vomit. With such small, isolated doses of birth-control pills (we're talking about just four to eight pills here), such risks as breast or uterine cancer simply don't exist. Granted, such a dosage isn't necessarily good for a conceptus. In the instances where the pregnancy is ongoing (usually this would happen only if the pills weren't taken within seventy-two hours of intercourse), we wouldn't insist on a surgical procedure but we certainly would make women aware of the possibility that the conceptus could be affected adversely if the method failed and a pregnancy ensued.

The upside is the fact that such emergency birth-control is astonishingly simple. It can be done cooperatively, with both sexual partners making the decision. It also can be done unilaterally, with the woman keeping the option of simply not divulging that there may have been a potential for a pregnancy. In either case, no one would ever even have to be burdened with wondering whether a pregnancy occurred. The treatment could be viewed simply as a precautionary measure—quite literally a morning-after solution. It's something anybody can do and any physician can—or should be able to—prescribe. In my more perfect world, the emergency birth-control kits would be stocked in the stores right next to the condoms, which would be on the racks next to the checkout counter where they couldn't be missed. Better still, all birth-control devices would be available on anonymous demand at dispensaries that never closed. I must emphasize that this is *emergency* contraception and that to simply use this after every episode of unprotected intercourse actually counterintuitively increases the failure rate to unacceptable levels. Because of the statistics of risk of pregnancy with each unprotected intercourse, ongoing contraception is much more effective.

But here's the more appalling aspect of the entire notion of emergency birth control: Relatively few health-care professionals even know about it. I hear from them some vague awareness that maybe there's some "morning-after" method awaiting FDA approval or that it involves some exotic medication about which they aren't quite aware. What it means to women looking for enlightenment and advice is an ongoing, off-putting, negative message. It's the sort of denial that perpetuates ideas about sex and pregnancy being something forbidden or unspeakable, dirty and wrong. At a time when society can benefit most from openness and shared, accurate information about sex and pregnancy, instead there seems to be an invisible embargo on useful information. When your own physician can't or won't give you the information you need, the problem involves more than simply finding another physician. It means that yet another doctor is presuming to practice medicine without being capable of helping a patient with a genuine health-care concern. If physicians don't know about a morning-after birth-control remedy, one might also wonder what else they don't know.

Such reticence has never been a problem for me. No matter what medical subject I'm asked to address and no matter what the forum, I will somehow find a way to draw the idea of emergency birth control into the discussion. People need to have this information. I've even been known to bring it up out of context, speaking on a supposedly unrelated subject and, as an aside, suddenly saying: "By the way, did you know that most physicians haven't the foggiest idea about emergency birth control?" In fact, the lack of knowledge is so pervasive in medicine that it's difficult for me to believe that it isn't part of some political design. It's hard for me to believe that the withholding of this knowledge isn't intentional in some way. If not, then what could possibly be the explanation for such a lack of knowledge? It's one of the most fascinating questions surrounding reproductive rights today.

In a more enlightened society there would be public-service commercials demonstrating emergency birth control. "Condom broke last night? Didn't remember to use one? Not ready for pregnancy? There's a kit waiting for you at your nearest drug or grocery store." This much I can guarantee: If they know nothing else by the time they leave my clinic, women are aware of the morning-after method. Knowledge is an empowering commodity. But trying to project onto society at large the policy of openness that prevails at my clinic seems unfathomable right now. This was—and in some areas remains—a nation in which many took great offense at even the most innocuous of public-service commercials about condom use. The double standard is that Americans will heap great viewer interest on all manner of sexual content: the titillation value of soap operas, for example, or the voyeuristic outlet of talk shows. But just try to slip in a subtle (much less a not so subtle) message about a condom that can save lives and protect against unwanted pregnancies. You'd think such messages amounted to some sinister conspiracy.

Instead, let's talk about a conspiracy of silence. It's the one that prevents the manufacturers of birth-control pills from even mentioning to doctors that the pills are effective as a morning-after method. Because such pills have not been approved by the FDA specifically for the use I've described, the drug companies are prevented from informing their customers of this potential benefit. How then can I recommend birth-control pills for morning-after treatment? According to FDA instructions, if a drug has been approved by the FDA for any reason, and a physician happens to use that drug for another purpose with the belief that the drug will have a beneficial effect, then the physician is permitted to do so. But the manufacturer can't advertise a drug for a purpose other than that for which it's been approved. Does this make sense? Not in the case of morning-after treatment.

I was encouraged not long ago when lecturing to a group of about seventy second-year medical students to find that about 80 percent were aware of the morning-after method. Most of them had not been aware of it prior to medical school, and all of them were part of a select group predisposed to care about abortion procedures. But I still found 80 percent to be quite high. I only wish the general population was similarly well informed. That would be particularly welcome in the case of young people, who know so much about other aspects of society but know relatively little about matters affecting their own bodies. I'll wager, for example, that more middle-school students have a much greater awareness about where to find alcohol, tobacco, drugs, and guns than they do about the facts behind pregnancy and birth control.

Using emergency birth control assumes that women are sure to be aware of when they've engaged in sex likely to lead to pregnancy. At best, such awareness would only be a highly educated guess. I can say this speaking as one who, after all, denied the signs of pregnancy well into my second term. There are women who tell us: "Oh, yes, I knew right away." Maybe they did, but I'm not sure how. Better, one would think, to go on the assumption that the conditions were right for conception and that it won't hurt to be on the safe side by taking the extra birth-control pills. I think if more people knew about the method they would simply say to themselves: "Look, I'm not waiting to see if I have a period when there's a 97 percent chance of assuring it if I take extra pills."

As far as birth control in general, there seems to be little on the horizon that is new. There may be some more work on specific inhibitors and antagonists, or blockers such as Mifepristone. As they exist now, the various methods of birth control are selected for reasons that differ with each woman. Those who don't like the idea of chemicals in their systems might be less inclined to take pills. If you don't like medicine in your system, then you're also not going to want Norplant or Depoprovera. That leaves as an alternative the so-called barrier methods: caps, diaphragms, foam and condoms. Maybe this also includes IUDs, although a lot of women who don't want chemicals in their bodies also don't want copper. The least intrusive birth-control method in terms of what goes into your system is something called a fertility-awareness method, which involves a backup use of foam and condoms during the time when the woman is fertile. This requires a tremendous amount of self-education about cycles as well as self-examinations. It obviously means a lot of time commitment: checking all the time, having to think a lot about your body. People like me who are highly motivated and educated about not getting pregnant also may be too distracted to check their fertility every day. I'm also someone brought up in a medical model (as opposed to someone not medically trained), with the belief that medicine is to be used toward good ends. I was someone who preferred birth-control pills for a number of years. Then I became so distracted with life and work that I couldn't be bothered to remember about taking birth-control pills. I went to the Depoprovera method, involving an injection every three months. I've also used an IUD, which worked fine except that my periods were a little heavier.

The first step, then, in making the birth-control decision involves the woman looking at her lifestyle as well as her beliefs and her level of comfort with her body. The next series of steps will be based on side effects perceived from the specific method selected. One kind of pill may make the woman bleed early, in which case she'll try another kind of pill. Another might give her headaches or make her feel bloated or nauseated. If she still really likes birth-control pills, she'll work with her caregiver to find the one that causes the least in the way of side effects. If for some reason the pills cause major problems such as blood clots in the veins, then the woman needs to move to a nonhormonal method of contraception for a while. Once the clotting is healed, however, the woman can use Norplant or Depoprovera.

The next decision-making step has to do with the failure rate for the selected form of birth control. Some women will love the diaphragm or other barrier methods, but they'll also wind up having unplanned pregnancies roughly three times in two years, according to current statistics. Yet, being able to choose a method that makes her the most comfortable by using her own fund of information is the ideal. It's important to have a caregiver knowledgeable about all the options, at which point the woman can make her own decision. But there is another large group of women who leave the birth-control decisions to their health-care providers. This is a less than ideal approach because it tends to alienate the woman from the decision-making process.

Birth-control pills can affect women in unpredictable ways. As a physician I would like to say: "This is an estrogen-dominant birth-control pill. Therefore, if I have someone who normally gets really tender breasts and is kind of headachy and nauseated before her menstrual cycle when her estrogen levels are usually high, then I should prescribe a birth-control pill that's not estrogen dominant." But then when I put her on the nonestrogen-dominant pill she has the same side effects. The side effects that are described in the pharmaceutical literature may not work out the same for the individual woman. They may apply generally to, say, ten thousand women. But for the individual, I need to approach each on a case by case basis. The really drastic side effects, strokes and blood clots, are extremely rare. Physicians can't predict these cases ahead of time, except to say that women who are over age thirty-five and heavy smokers are more prone to such risks. Yet, more birth-control-pill-related strokes occur with women younger than thirty-five simply because we've concentrated our efforts on educating the heavy-smoking, over-thirty-five women about the risks.

The typical method of prescribing birth-control pills is to try women for two to three months on a particular kind, then have them come back and see how it worked out. It takes at least two or three menstrual cycles to determine how they will respond to a particular pill. Some women report changes in libido after taking birth-control pills. What isn't clear is whether increased or decreased libido is simply due to lack of concern about getting pregnant. What's more clear is that certain women's decreased libido can be the result of vaginal dryness sometimes brought on with Depoprovera. It's rare, but it does happen.

To what extent do women practice birth control? My belief is that it's nearly 100 percent. This means that when couples, for example, practice withdrawal, they honestly believe they're reducing the odds of unwanted pregnancies. And that, precisely, is the definition of birth control. It doesn't just mean condoms or pills. The "rhythm method" advocated by the Catholic church during its more enlightened moments is birth control. And, since withdrawal is a conscious effort to avoid pregnancy and achieve birth control, one begins to see what this says about the political discourse concerning the subject. Haven't Pat Robertson or Pat Buchanan or Phil Gramm ever—maybe just once—withdrawn during intercourse to avoid pregnancies? If so, then how can they rail against other forms of birth control—abortion included—without being hypocritical?

Then again, the hypocrisies of the patriarchy are an ongoing source of bemusement to feminist women. One might ask: What exactly is a "feminist" woman? The answer, as we'll see, is fairly simple. Where it gets complicated is in the increasingly familiar cases of conservative women refusing to accept the feminist label while enjoying precisely the lives that feminism wishes for all women.

18

The Backlash

Much of what Martha Stewart does—or says she does—is utterly unattainable during a 168-hour week. She is a feminist, however. She's an astute business woman selling a product that purports to be synonymous with ease and comfort but in fact does nothing but add another level of stress to the lives of many overextended women. Consider the message: You can whip up a gourmet dinner for twelve and serve it on your handmade linens decorated with your perfectly-arranged-in-three-minute flowers while wearing silk in your spotless kitchen. You can do this after having spent all day grubbing in the dirt to develop a picture-perfect garden fit for inspection by the "Today" program TV audience the following morning. It's certainly something I'll never attain. Martha Stewart has no dirty corners in her house. There are no piles of letters and clutter strewn about. She's stuck with the same twenty-four-hour day as the rest of us, so it's a wonder how she does it all. Something has to give. Maybe she doesn't read much.

Facetiousness aside, Martha Stewart is an industry. She obviously has a lot of help, as she no doubt would be the first to admit. But television viewers and readers of Stewart's magazine, *Martha Stewart's Living*, aren't privy to the less romantic, more prosaic aspects of the tasks she makes seem so easy. So maybe it will do to consider the Martha Stewart can-do philosophy in terms of the following statistic from a recent issue of the *Journal of the American Medical Women's Association*: 74 percent of female physicians do all their own domestic work such as cleaning, cooking, laundry, and child-rearing. The inference I draw is this: We liberated, educated women who have moved into these tremendously demanding careers outside of the home, in an effort to avoid being held accountable for something bad happening in the family, have been carrying all the domestic duties that we always have. Moreover, I can understand this because, although I have a housekeeper, I also am part of the statistic to some extent. For example, if something is happening with my children's schedule on a given day, chances are very good that I'll be the one making the accommodations, even though I happen to be married to an extraordinary partner. The Martha Stewart philosophy serves to remind women like me that, not only should we be brilliant and productive at work, we also should maintain these lovely homes and entertain lavishly on a regular basis. Somehow we should be expected to do all that men traditionally did and all that the so-called stay-at-home mothers did—and do it all in the same 168-hour week in which men perform their traditional duties.

It's a time of great change and thus a time of great stress for everyone. Considering how much different human existence has become in such a relatively brief time span, why shouldn't it be? During six hundred of the past eight hundred generations, people lived in caves without experiencing any change at all. Only the most recent fifty generations have been familiar with the written word. Just the past three or four generations have had electricity. Are we surprised that we're a little stressed out, then, when every year brings new technology to assimilate and less time to enjoy what we already have? There was electricity and phones, then cars and airplanes, space exploration, computers, virtual reality: all within about a century. The typical middle-class home has a dozen technology-related digital clocks, no two of them showing the same time. The microwave clock disagrees with the one on the VCR, which contradicts the coffee-pot timer, to say nothing of the alarm clocks in each bedroom. With all we've been learning to assimilate during the past few decades, now we're advised that we all should reserve an extra four waking hours a day for getting on-line and cruising the information highway. How could we not be stressed out?

On top of that there's the assumption by the patriarchy that the women of the world are trying to upset the power structure. This is a conscious and occasionally semiconscious backlash. Ironically, the degree of backlash against women's rights is itself a tremendous way to measure how much we've moved and how far we've come. Part of the backlash has been characterized by an attempt—overt at times, subtle at others—to divide feminists. This assertion says: "Feminists no longer comprise an open-door group of women. They reject one another for various reasons, and we always knew this would happen. Feminists are all divided now, with these really radical feminists insisting that nobody else is a true feminist. And for feminism to survive, feminists need to do this, this, and this so that all feminists will agree on every last detail of feminism." How ridiculous. A feminist is not necessarily a proponent of any philosophy beyond the belief that a woman should be treated like a human being. It's not only a simple, straightforward concept, it's also one that means anybody— men, women, and children—can be feminists. It means anybody who has ever preached or believed in the notion of equality for all people is by definition a feminist. That's all it is. It's about as inclusive as you can get. And a woman is called a feminist the day she decides that she no longer wants to be treated like a doormat. That's also pretty inclusive unless you happen to know of many women who actually enjoy being walked on.

A second aspect of the backlash is the attempt to clamp down on affirmative action. This is aimed at people of color as well as women. The patriarchal argument against affirmative action tends to ignore the threat to the white-male establishment. The benefit of getting rid of affirmative action, ironically, always is stated as the patriarchy feels it pertains to the ones who actually have gained from the practice. The patriarchy says the practice does an egregious disservice to women and minorities by telling them they'll never know if they have reached their position because of their talent and performance or because they happened to be part of a quota. One wonders at times why the patriarchy seems to feel so threatened. In fact, when you look at hiring numbers and the level of white males in positions of power, it doesn't appear that affirmative action has upset the preexisting balance all that much. When considering income statistics, it's pretty obvious that white males still command a lot more pay than women or minorities. But we've somehow given the perception that we've taken white-male places, and this has provoked a lot of anger among less well-educated white males. The truth is that we haven't achieved anything resembling the power of the patriarchy—and it doesn't appear that we will anytime soon. Moreover, who ever said certain jobs and roles and positions of power were reserved for white males? Even if the world were to grant power based on size of population, white males could make no claim to power. The fact is that there are more Asian women in the world than Caucasian men.

A third part of the backlash has to do with the Catholic church and fundamentalist groups, including members of the antichoice movement saying they're concerned about babies not being born when what they're really concerned with is keeping women in their place. If women are moving out of the home and into professional careers, then they can't be kept subjugated the way they were during past generations. Empowering women constitutes a tremendous threat to the old power structures of the patriarchal institutions. These institutions, including most corporations, have much to gain from maintaining a status quo in which women assume the secondary roles once accepted as "traditional." But even fundamentalists at the "bubba" level, many of whom surfaced during the recent militia hysteria spawned by the Oklahoma City bombing, are mortally afraid of women in power. At a gun-show gathering in New Hampshire in 1995, the T-shirt of one of the participants seemed to sum up the philosophy at the lower end of the patriarchy. It read: "God, Guns and Guys."

Yet another part of the backlash against feminism has to do with elevating and exaggerating our accomplishments. This philosophy poses the rhetorical question: "What are women whining about? Look at them marching wool-suit clad through the cities. Look at the superstar clout of Barbra Streisand and Demi Moore. Women have arrived. They've gotten everything they need to get." Have we? Not in equal pay we haven't. Not in equal distribution of domestic responsibilities. Most poverty-level families are headed by single women. Women have no real legal recourse against domestic violence. Moreover, we haven't even achieved equality in a lot of cases involving elite institutions where money is supposed to be the sole qualifier. A *New York Times* story in early 1995 told of how women fare at golf clubs. If there's a divorce and remarriage, the new wife is added to the club membership. The ex-wife, if she wants to continue as a member, has to reapply, pay the entry fees, and still may not be able to get in.

But inequities are global. In Beijing where the 1995 international women's conference was held, the nongovernmental organizations had been welcomed and the Chinese government had agreed to make all the accommodations in Beijing. Then they learned who these women were and what their politics were and all bets were off. A place was provided but it was forty miles outside of Beijing, with no water, no phones, no hotels. When the organizers of the event protested, an offer was made to put up tents for them. This was for a major international meeting about women's rights. Imagine if it had been an international trade conference with mostly men. Would the delegates have been consigned to a tent city? With no water or electricity? Does a tent city outside of the mainstream constitute "everything we need to get"?

Can it be asserted, then, that a monolithic opposition to women's rights exists? No, it's factionalized. It ranges, here again, from mindless white-male gun toters to male-dominated religious organizations to CEOs of major corporations. Each feels it has a vested interest in keeping women subjugated. Each acts individually. But the general philosophy is pervasive: "Women are the nurturers. They have times of the month when they don't make decisions very well. They're not very strong physically. They don't think in a linear fashion. They're incapable of supervising other workers. They belong at home. They aren't as smart. They're not as good as men at math and science." If you've been brought up with these unifying themes of the patriarchal system, then chances are you believe such ideas and are likely to perpetuate them. Men, because they could see the advantages that accrued from believing these things, would be more likely to adhere to these beliefs than women. But certain women with low self-esteem find little difficulty going along with this view when told by men either directly or in subtle ways that they are inferior.

Have women entered enough positions of power as of 1996 to successfully fend off the backlashes from the patriarchy? Yes and no. We haven't achieved enough positions of power to fend them off entirely. But we will manage to keep the movement going. There aren't yet enough women in infrastructural rather than token positions. This is especially true after the 1994 elections, which resulted in fewer women in positions of political power. The irony is that many of the newly elected women are conservatives vocally opposed to feminism while living and embodying feminist ideals. They do a job as well as a male, receive equal pay, are away from home, and are in the public eye looking and acting smart. Linda Smith, the right-wing fundamentalist who defeated Jolene Unsoeld for a U.S. congressional seat from Washington State, stoutly refuses to be seen as a feminist. But of course she's a feminist. Or, if not, does she believe that a woman shouldn't be treated like a human being? Would she accept less political power in the U.S. Congress than a male member? Would she take less pay? Would she, by our definition, allow herself to be treated like a doormat? Of course she wouldn't. But Smith and other conservative women in Congress willingly go along with a political agenda that would jeopardize women's rights. Does that make them hypocrites or stupid or both? Linda Smith, along with Helen Chenoweth of Idaho and other staunch right-wing women, get to live the feminist life, but they didn't have to fight for the rights that were hard won by the rest of us. These women are shortsighted enough to help pass laws that will, ironically, endanger the very feminist lives that they enjoy. From their positions of relative safety amid the patriarchy, they'll have no qualms about denying other women affirmative-action opportunities or curbing abortion rights. Do they feel this will get them admitted to the patriarchy? And is this what they really desire?

If so, then they're woefully shortsighted. Then again, shortsightedness can easily afflict those with money and jobs and power. Their power secures their rights. The assumption—conscious or not—is either that the loss of rights never will happen to them or that a double standard is appropriate. The double standard says that it's all right for the Linda Smiths and Helen Chenoweths and Phyllis Schlaflys to have lives and careers outside of the home. But other women need to stay back and be barefoot, pregnant servants of the patriarchy.

The double standard and the hypocrisy of such women having it both ways is outrageous. One way of getting around it, as I've found, is simply to live your politics and believe your politics. One of the ideas for which the feminist movement can claim responsibility is that the political is the personal and vice versa. I found myself asking: What do I do about what I perceive to be the world political situation? Given that I lack supreme political authority, what can I do to make my little corner of the world a feminist world? A lot, actually. In my little corner of the world, for example, we don't use terrible chemicals. We don't hate people because their opinions differ from ours. We don't subscribe to a patriarchal attitude that finds no problem with subjugating half the population on the basis of sex. None of these is going to have any great effect on the world. Relatively speaking, the effects will be tiny. But that's okay. If a tiny effect is the best that I can cause, then fine. It allows me to believe truly that I live my politics. So I left family medicine and became strictly an abortion provider on the basis of personal politics. I viewed it as politically unfair to me that women should be forced to bear babies if they don't choose to. Another conscious decision is to rear feminist sons. That's what can result when you really live and think your politics, when you truly spend time reading and worrying about the world.

So, lacking the patience or the stomach for elective office, I have to continue to resolve to maintain my own little corner of the world. At times it can seem a decidedly isolated world, too. My sons have asked on occasion, for example, why it is that they sometimes find themselves being the only prochoice kids in a group when the subject of abortion comes up. The reason, as they have come to realize, is that the way we think is politically the right way for us to think about these matters, even if—especially if—prochoice ideas are challenged by peers. It is good and right and necessary for us to speak out when we disagree with others even if doing so is unpopular.

Having said that, my sons might have been just as liable to be little patriarchs in the making had they not been shown a better way to view women and support human rights. It would be comforting to suppose that the old-line members of the patriarchy are going to die off naturally some day and that we will make generational progression. But I see budding little patriarchs out there all the time. In the absence of proper education, they see nothing wrong with growing up to subjugate women because this is something that has been institutionalized in American society.

Yet, hard as it may be to imagine, there are greater problems for women, and they all come down to one word: Money.

19

I Never Thought About It That Way

There is a problem besides the ongoing threat to reproductive rights that is of paramount concern to women, and it has to do directly with the freedom of choice. The problem is the inability of women to achieve financial equality with men. Money is power in this country and many of America's social problems stem from the fact that women simply do not have anything approaching an equal financial power base. Achieving that equality has been and will continue to be difficult. Because it is threatening to a lot of men to imagine women attaining economic equality, a lot of women are going to be beaten up emotionally and physically on the road toward their goal.

Think of the consequences for many women who lack an equal financial power base. Let's say a woman upsets her male partner and does something that might result in her getting beat up. She can't leave the man because she doesn't have any financial options beyond living with him. That's the main reason women in shelters give for having put up with abusive situations. They simply couldn't afford to take their children and leave. With the Republican plans for cutting welfare payments, women living near the poverty level will have even fewer options, as will the working poor. As to the latter, women will continue to make up most of the working-poor population because women at every socioeconomic level continue to suffer the same pay inequities. Every study has shown that the vast majority of women can't make dollar-for-dollar what men do for the same work.

Many in this country seem to have a tremendous problem with the providing of equal opportunities. The sad irony is that access to opportunity in itself can go a long way toward curbing the kind of violence that virtually everybody seems to abhor. Reducing violence—especially against women—is not going to come about until the haves and the have-nots share the incredible wealth in this country. Redistribution of wealth, of course, is among the greatest fears of conservatives because they view it as handing over the power that rich people hold over the poor. As it is, our country suffers from a great undercurrent of hatred and resentment—"us versus them"—based on one side not having enough and the other having too much. If there were more equal access to education so that there was greater parity in people's incomes, then there would be perforce less violence. If there were jobs for everybody, if wealth were shared more equitably, then much of the resentment and anger would immediately dissipate. But what I see in the near future is just the opposite. As welfare is dismantled there will be more violence and poverty that will affect women more adversely than men. At the other extreme, women who are achieving wealth and power will continue to maintain a level of power that will make it impossible for the patriarchy to keep them down. Some of the laws and regulations in place are so good that there will, for example, be more and more equity in women's sports. I'd like to feel that it will become increasingly difficult to keep women out of high management positions, but I see no strong evidence that this is more than a wish. Where we seem to be in this country is stuck in the same kind of fin de siècle angst that prevailed here at the ends of prior centuries. In my more optimistic moments I actually believe that the attacks on affirmative action will be unsuccessful. If they do succeed, the result will be the further institutionalization of discriminatory practices. Under affirmative action it's been difficult enough for the previously powerless to advance. Without affirmative action there would be no pressure whatsoever on employers and institutions to consider hiring, appointing, or promoting women and minorities.

All of the challenges to women, then, add up to the continuing importance of maintaining and strengthening reproductive rights. If women are in for a backlash that will make their lives more difficult, then there will be all the more reason for them to have the ability to abort unwanted pregnancies and avoid having children they can't possibly take care of. Indeed, the antichoice crowd may already have found itself forming an unofficial (and one would have thought improbable) coalition with feminists over the welfare-reform issue. Many antiabortion people see through the fallacy of the proposition that if you don't give a woman any money, then she will realize it is in her best interest not to have any more babies and she won't become pregnant anymore. The facts are that (a) women don't "get pregnant" without the obvious participation of men, many of whom have shown little regard for the financial consequences of a pregnancy, and (b) there is no information to suggest that a lack of money ever reduced the number of pregnancies. But the inability to support children can lead to the seeking of abortions. Being aware of this, the antichoice side also is aware that the lack of money from welfare may yet prompt growing numbers of poor pregnant women to seek abortions. That, in turn, couldn't help but strengthen the already considerable prochoice sentiment in this country, and that, of course, would weaken the appeal of the antichoice persuasion. Some conservative discourse of early 1995 already has resulted in politicians talking out of both sides of their mouths. On the one hand, they'd love to end welfare because of the perception that it eventually would end the existence of the cliché "welfare mother." On the other hand, they know that they dare not cause too much more poverty and hopelessness for fear of the spectacle of pregnant poor women storming the abortion clinics demanding help. Wouldn't all this be made easier simply by giving poor people true opportunities to better themselves? Do conservative politicians really believe that women in great numbers enjoy participating in the welfare-poverty cycle? Don't these conservatives have any regard for the notion of redemption of spirit through the dignity of work?

Another ludicrous assumption about ending welfare is that men won't want their partners to get pregnant if they know the women won't subsequently receive welfare money. Now there's an argument. Here we have young men, many of them in the poorest urban areas, boasting about "tagging" young women, which is to say, getting them pregnant. Someone please explain to me how such macho mindlessness suddenly is going to change simply by taking away the prospect of welfare benefits. Are we to blame these young men? Maybe to an extent we are. On the other hand, would they behave this way had they been exposed to decent male role models during their formative years? There emphatically are good male role models for poor young men. But there are far fewer than there should be, and the reason has everything to do with the fact that there aren't nearly enough good jobs to make poverty-prone families stable. If we want to perpetuate proper role-modeling, then let's help the less well off attain the dignity of work. If we want to achieve genuine "family values" (as opposed to the right-wing "values" touted by a patriarchy bent on subjugating women), we don't need to preach to poor people, many of whom demonstrate better social values than their wealthier counterparts. But first they have to have the financial stability that gives them the luxury of taking time for the consideration of values. That time is a luxury usually afforded only to those who have taken care of life's other pressing needs.

We see documentary evidence of the failure of poor families, and it's pretty hard to miss the economic component of the failure. It happens, for example, in the widely acclaimed film *Hoop Dreams*.

One of the families has a home and stability until the father loses his job. Then everything starts to collapse because (a) there isn't any reserve to fall back on and (b) there isn't another job to turn to. Conservatives argue that there indeed is an abundance of jobs. Possibly. But they're all service jobs at minimum wage and no one can live on such incomes, let alone support anybody else. But then we speak of raising the minimum wage. I'd immediately take it past $7 an hour. And how is this greeted by conservatives? This can't be done because employers would go broke. We're to believe that McDonald's and Burger King couldn't pass along to consumers enough of the burden required to ease the financial plight of the working poor? Phil Gramm, the noted economics professor and presidential candidate, says categorically that to raise the minimum wage even to five bucks an hour would be the ruin of businesses everywhere. It wouldn't occur to him that paying an honest wage for honest labor might instead engender the dignity that would result in greater loyalty and productivity. It's beyond the ken of such a noted public figure that rewarding labor actually could result in greater incomes for businesses because of the rise in productivity.

Liberal economic arguments have fallen so far out of favor in this country that one is obliged to feel like a heretic even articulating them. And who loses? Low-income wage earners, most of them women.

I was asked not long ago whether help for women would result from the election of a woman president. It would depend on the woman. If it were, say, Linda Smith, then the answer obviously would be no. As a practical matter, an extremist such as Smith never could be elected president here. But let's say for the sake of argument that the near future brought an electable woman whose politics fell somewhere between the Democrat Dianne Feinstein and the Republican Christine Whitman. Let me start by noting that the more women who are elected to office in representational government, the better the results overall for women. But a single-event woman president? I doubt that there's much she could accomplish in four years. If she shared a party majority in both houses of Congress and had been elected in a landslide, which is probably impossible, then I suppose she could make a major impact. But I honestly believe that the trickle up is going to work better for women than the trickle down. For each woman to constantly aim higher and higher in what she's doing will eventually make it easier for younger women coming along. This is to say that by the time it has become routine to have women in the Senate and in high-level cabinet posts and on presidential tickets, it will become much less difficult for the electorate to accept the notion of a woman as president. Beyond that, even as chief executive, it's not as though a woman could bring about such reforms as earnings equity. A president, after all, is politically shackled. Besides, if a woman president were to do something dramatically liberal she'd run a much greater risk of being assassinated. Think of the loathing fringe groups harbor for Janet Reno, who always is mentioned second to Bill Clinton on the hate lists of militia leaders and talk-radio fanatics. The enmity has less to do with any Reno role in the Branch Davidian incident in Waco than with the fact that she's a strong, assertive, effective woman leader.

We also have the examples of women who have risen to the positions of Supreme Court justices. What makes this so important for women in general is that with Sandra Day O'Connor and Ruth Bader Ginsburg performing well—as they do—on the Court, suddenly it seems much more plausible to accept women for appointments to lesser judgeships across the country. Judgeships are excellent positions from which to create and enforce favorable results for women, assuming that the female judges are policy-making feminists rather than conservatives. One of the subtle advantages of having a liberal presidential administration is that women of more progressive outlooks are given such bench appointments in much greater numbers. But a more obvious feminist advantage of having women on the Supreme Court or in high-level cabinet posts is that such appointments reinforce for younger women the notion that there are fewer barriers to their advancement. These are young women who already have seen that it is preposterous to imagine that they couldn't go to law or medical school. They scarcely can believe there was a time when women's sports programs weren't widely available in schools. That level of disbelief is itself extremely heartening because it tells us there's absolutely no way women in this country ever would go back to a patriarchal system that kept them from pursuing such goals.

I believe that the abortion issue can never regress to a point where it would be made illegal again. Too many women—and a lot of men—simply wouldn't stand for it. It's too well accepted. Too many women have had to use it in their times of need. Too many women have discovered that their politics change when their situations change; and though they may have once thought abortion was wrong, they are persuaded to a prochoice position when the need arises for them or a loved one to end an unwanted pregnancy. I'm also mildly optimistic that domestic violence against women can be curbed. This can happen, here again, if we approach a level of financial equity. It can happen when, for example, men and children come to the understanding that the responsibility for maintaining a household doesn't belong to the woman of the house but to everybody who benefits from living there. Violence will be curbed when boys and young men are taught that when somebody makes you mad, you talk about it rather than engage in physical combat. It will happen when grownups and peers refuse to praise young men and boys for punching somebody. We can only make those changes one family at a time. What it requires is an intact family living above the poverty level so that the family members can think about what to do when a violent crisis occurs. Instead we have impoverished areas where the daily reality includes substandard nutrition, no prospects for betterment, and—worst of all—the constant threat of violence. On the parental level, there's simply no energy left to deal with the escalating violence in a way that will benefit society at large. So the violence increases unabated. This is because you have to be living at a level above mere survival in order to deal with those finer points in life. And isn't it a logical hypothesis that there would be much less domestic violence in places such as Sweden, France, and Denmark, where the vast majority of the population had progressed well beyond the level of subsistence living? How did those places get to that level of social well-being? The answer is: by promoting the notion of economic equity.

It would be good to believe that by laying out my so-called liberal ideas I could persuade everybody about their merits. Obviously it doesn't work that way. I understand this whenever I get into a discussion with those who believe passionately in a conservative agenda. But what can possibly be an argument against, say, the Head Start program? Here is an entry system to civilization in which children come into a program and are told specifically by Head Start teachers that "these are the rules of the classroom, and we deal with problems in these ways." Every single child in this country should go through Head Start. And beyond that there should be comprehensive life-skills classes taught at all levels by responsible human beings. As it is, though, you try to teach a responsible course to sixth-graders about the ways boys and girls interact, and suddenly there's some fundamentalist Christian ranting about the wrath of God.

I have noted that I listen to the impassioned opinions of conservatives. That could lead one to wonder, then, how I could possibly sit still and listen to someone who advocates the benefits to be gained by subjugating women. Obviously I abhor such a belief. But I also know precisely what such a patriarchal position means. To certain people—mostly men—it makes great good sense to subjugate women. Their point is that it's obviously much easier to live when you can depend on riding on the back of somebody who is taking care of all your domestic needs and physical comforts. As the Mary Chapin Carpenter lyric sarcastically echoes the old condescending TV commercial: "He thinks he'll keep her." "Keeping" a de facto slave is, from a certain patriarchal perspective, totally logical. It makes perfect sense. A lot of men never could have reached the lofty positions they now enjoy had it not been for the existence of the women who served them all their lives. If I were a patriarch, I'd be extremely threatened by feminism. It would be precisely the same as the threat felt by slave-holders prior to the Civil War. Women as slaves to the patriarchy? Yes, and in some often hilarious ways. Think of Michael Huffington, the California conservative who tried to spend his way into Dianne Feinstein's Senate seat in 1994. This man had no campaign to offer other than some vague "family-values" agenda. When he finally conceded the loss months after the election, Huffington added to the embarrassment caused by his prolonged, pathetic challenge by responding to a cocktail-party query about the identity of his child's private school. Unable to come up with the name of the school, this titan of family values suggested that the person inquiring go ask Huffington's wife, because "she'll know." He thinks he'll keep her. Michael Huffington, like other patriarchs, knows that life runs much more smoothly if you have a servant. Slavery had a lengthy and tenacious history for some very compelling, if eminently despicable, reasons. The key reason was simply that many white people concluded that it was cheaper and easier to live if the slave did the work. By the same token, it would be of great comfort to the patriarchy to believe that women would willfully and in great numbers go back to being even more slavish for men than they are now.

Perhaps certain patriarchs held out such a hope during the mid-1980s. Let's recall, after all, that there was a time not very many years ago when we were reading about how young women were repudiating feminism. The idea was that they were somehow concerned that young men wouldn't like them if they asserted their equality. They wouldn't be "popular." In retrospect it was nothing but another attempt to divide women. The message was: "See! It's not working! You women just can't work together. Your thinking differs from the way that other group of women is thinking." In fact, I've observed that if you take a given group of five young women and five middle-aged women, they get along very well together and the concerns they express are very similar. But a decade ago there was a great hoopla made about what a few women thought was a negative connotation of feminism. It was the idea that "guys won't dig us if they think we're feminists." There was something strategically similar working among certain young men, whose attitude was: "Women will dig us if they think we're feminists." The guys may well be budding patriarchs posing as feminists. There are plenty of men who seem to be sympathetic to feminism but would turn on us the moment their jobs were threatened. But I'll gladly take these guys over true-blue patriarchs any day, because at least I can talk with the posers. I made a conscious political decision a long time ago: Attitude changes take generations and behavioral changes take very little time. I'll take someone whose behavior is changing—maybe he's stopped calling women "bitches"—with the hope that eventually it will lead to a change in attitude. In the case of young people's attitudes toward feminism, much of what both young women and men were doing got down to the kind of insecurity spawned by semantics. The very notion of "feminist" had somehow become synonymous in some circles with "socialist," "Marxist," "no makeup," "homosexual," or "butch." It was a very effective antifeminist methodology that no doubt emboldened the likes of Rush Limbaugh, who eventually would refer to any person who asserted equal rights for women as a "feminazi." Think of all this labeling in terms of the sensibility of a typical heterosexual teenage young woman. Her body is changing and she's thinking about what's going to happen to her sexually and socially. She desperately wants to be accepted by her peers when along comes this terribly negative connotation about what is meant by being a "feminist." The pressure to reject such a label could be enormous.

There also has been a trend toward factionalization at the top echelon of the women's movement. Spokeswomen ranging from Naomi Wolfe—is she too fluffy?—to Camille Paglia—is she too butch?—have emerged. The top-level spokeswomen seem to be at odds with one another. But then in talking with regular folks it occurs that we aren't necessarily so factionalized. When women get together and talk about what they believe, it becomes clear that there's a lot more commonality than would seem to be the case based on what is being said by the apparent celebrities of the movement. Moreover, it doesn't make any difference whether feminists disagree on certain philosophical points. Rather than proceed from some centralized, dictatorial set of feminist dogma, it's vastly more important for each woman to establish a feminist bubble that surrounds her. These women will affect everyone with whom they live and associate, and that for me is far more beneficial than the existence of any card-carrying membership in any single political group. But the microcosm of the individual and the macrocosm of the group are so enmeshed that it can be hard to maintain that individual bubble of feminism without the existence of the larger political group from which to draw energy and inspiration.

So let's encourage feminists to argue with one another. Patriarchs, after all, have argued with each other for centuries and it hasn't weakened them one whit. Even with so many men having been persuaded to the human-rights sense of feminism, I don't anticipate seeing the death throes of the American patriarchy any time soon. As for other countries, imagine the difficulty of being a feminist in, say, Liberia or Afghanistan or China. What a strong, brave woman it must take to be a feminist in those places, where women's rights advocates can scarcely afford the luxury of arguing among one another for fear of weakening their already tenuous position amid the patriarchy.

But in America, let's argue, and let's switch the emphasis to a celebration of the diversity of ideas. It's all right for us to say: It's wonderful that so many different political systems can exist within the feminist movement. It's a sign of intellectual progress that one feminist can say she believes in A and B but not C, while another subscribes to B and C and not A. Instead, the patriarchy chooses to characterize it as women who can't even get along among themselves! It's that sort of attitude that tells me feminists in America, while having made genuine progress, haven't seriously weakened the power of the patriarchy.

Then again, I choose to look toward the progress. That's a major reason for this book. It's an acknowledgment of what I've observed while personally interacting with more than two thousand women at my clinic every year: evidence that many have decided to think about what feminism means and what the patriarchy believes. Every once in a while a woman will pause after considering what it means to make the simple demand to be treated like an equal human being. Then she'll look up and say to me: "You know, Dr. Poppema, I never thought about it that way before."

It's a great triumph for them and for me an ongoing cause for hope.

Appendix A

AURORA MEDICAL SERVICES
SEATTLE, WASHINGTON

Name _____ Date of Birth ____ Today's Date ___

1. I authorize Dr. _____ to treat the following condition, which has been explained to me: Pregnancy, which is to be terminated.

2. I consent to the administration of anesthesia by my attending physician.

3. I recognize that during the course of treatment, unforeseen conditions may require additional or different procedures. I authorize my attending physician to perform these procedures as required by his or her professional judgment.

4. I recognize that there are risks associated with any minor surgical procedure, including suction or sharp curettage of the uterus, and unforeseen complications may arise which require additional treatment or hospitalization at my own expense. I acknowledge that no guarantee has been made to me as to the result and that I have been informed of the possible complications which include, but are not limited to:

Infection
False positive pregnancy test
Failure of the procedure to end the pregnancy
Undetectable tubal pregnancy (ectopic)
Allergic reaction to medications or anesthesia which could include cardiac arrest, brain damage or death
Retained Tissue
Excessive blood loss
Laceration or perforation of the cervix or uterus

These complications could result in the need to repeat the procedure, hospitalization, additional surgery, blood transfusion, permanent disability, or permanent sterility. I understand that the complication and fatality rate for this type of procedure is much less than the complication and fatality rate for term pregnancy and delivery.

5. I understand the importance of returning to the clinic for my post-abortion checkup within two to three weeks of the procedure.

6. I understand that in case of emergency I am to return to the clinic if possible or go to the nearest emergency room for care.

7. I understand that in the instance of emergency treatment or hospitalization, parental consent may become inevitable.

8. I understand that pregnancy tissue and parts will be removed during this procedure, and I consent to their examination and disposal by any attending physician.

9. I certify that my attending physician has informed me of the nature of treatment and of the anticipated result; of possible risks, complications, and benefits of treatment; and of alternate treatments, including non-treatment.

10. I certify that I have read or had read to me the contents of this form. I have read or had read to me and will abide by the postoperative instructions for this procedure. I understand the risks involved in this type of surgical procedure and have decided to proceed with surgery after considering the possibility of both known and unknown complications. I attest that I have had the opportunity to ask questions and all of my questions have been answered to my satisfaction.

Signature _____ Witness _____ Date _____

Appendix B

Date: _____ Name: _____

AURORA MEDICAL SERVICES
Seattle, Washington

The first part of your visit to Aurora Medical Services will be spent with a counselor. She will be talking with you about any issues or concerns important to you, as well as going over your medical history, the abortion procedure, a consent form, birth control information, and after care instructions. In order for your counselor to address what is most important to you, please answer the following questions by circling the response that most accurately describes your feelings.

1. How are you feeling about your decision to have an abortion?
   a. Very comfortable
   b. Somewhat comfortable
   c. Very uncomfortable

2. How are you feeling about the safety of abortion?
   a. Not at all concerned
   b. Somewhat concerned
   c. Very concerned

3. What are your thoughts about how you will feel during the abortion?
   a. Not at all concerned
   b. Somewhat concerned
   c. Very concerned

4. What are your thoughts about how you will feel after your abortion?
   a. Not at all concerned
   b. Somewhat concerned
   c. Very concerned

5. How much support do you have from others in relation to your decision?
   a. Lots of support
   b. Some support
   c. No support at all

Please tell us of any other issues you would like to discuss.

_____

_____

Many patients have found it helpful to see the fetal tissue after their abortion. If you feel this would be beneficial to you, please feel free to discuss this with your counselor.

Are you interested in seeing the fetal tissue after your abortion?

YES   NO   MAYBE

Appendix C

Sheryl Knowlen (her last name has been altered, as are the names of the other women in the appendices) is a Seattle community organizer who sought a Mifepristone abortion at our clinic in February 1995. The thirty-four-year-old college graduate also consented to be the subject of a video documentary that would be aired nationally. Following are Knowlen's comments about her background (which includes three surgical abortions) and her experience with the drug-induced abortion.

"I'm as fertile as the plains of Kansas," she said, regarding her four pregnancies that ended in abortion.

She recalled that in 1980 she was achieving birth control by using an IUD.

"I was 19, and for some reason I suppose I thought I couldn't get pregnant," she said.

Knowlen had recently broken off a relationship in Florida. Arriving in Seattle, she discovered she was pregnant. That led to an abortion at the clinic operated at the time by Dr. George Denniston.

"My next pregnancy was in Denmark, before I was twenty-two," she said. "It was the only time in my life that I was truly careless about having sex, and I got pregnant again."

She recalled that the Denmark procedure called for "putting me out" with medication. She also was required to stay over one night in a hospital.

"The interesting thing with Denmark," Knowlen said, "was the approach to birth control. My doctor was pretty arrogant with me. In Denmark, people get birth control information in high school, and I guess the doctor just expected me to know about it. She was quite snooty about the whole thing. It was as though, if I hadn't gotten the information by then, it was too late. In Europe they just don't make such a big deal about sex and birth control. They're much more open about reproductive rights. When my sister-in-law from Eastern Europe visited here, she said: 'You Americans are so strange. You sell everything in this country with sex, everything from cars to laundry detergent, but I can't take my shirt off at the beach without causing a big stir.' "

Knowlen's third pregnancy, she said, was the result of "my cervical cap falling off. I did all the things you're supposed to do when that happens: use more spermicide, put the thing back on. But I knew I was pregnant. I just had that feeling. A couple of weeks later I was in Holland and I asked a friend if there was a clinic around. She said there was an abortion clinic just around the corner. I walked over in the pouring rain and they wanted to know how late I thought I was. I told them it probably wasn't more than a week or so, that I'd been traveling. Then I got out my calendar and realized two of the weekly pages were stuck together, so I was a week farther along than I thought. I ended up going in for the abortion that afternoon.

"That one was really sad," she said, referring to the waiting room at the clinic. "In a lot of different parts of southern Europe, reproductive rights are much more restricted than in northern Europe.

The mixture of faces I saw in the waiting room was really interesting. I saw some people who looked like they were from northern Africa, I heard some Spanish-speaking people."

The inference she drew was that it was easier for such women to go to Amsterdam for an abortion than it was to seek such a procedure at home.

"It's the same as how it was before abortion was legal here," she surmised. "People scraped up the money and went to New York. There were a lot of very worried-looking people at the clinic in Holland."

She recalled that the demeanor at the clinic was "very businesslike." In the operating room, she said, there were metal carts with the sterilized surgical equipment rolled up like place-settings in a restaurant.

Later she kept the experience private, refusing to discuss it with traveling companions. She also split up with her partner.

"He'd grown up Catholic. All summer while I was gone I tried to find the words to write to him and explain what had happened. Instead, I waited until I got back.

"I want kids," Knowlen insisted. "But I've seen what it can do—and I'm not saying it isn't right, but that it wasn't right for me in certain instances. You wind up changing the direction of your life because you have a child rather than having a child to fit into your life and enrich it. Maybe that's my mid-nineties selfish streak, but I feel very strongly about having a planned kid. And I don't want to raise a kid alone."

She said that it may yet prove that she'll have a child that isn't planned, but that her ideal remains finding a life partner and planning a child together.

"I lost my job at the end of December [1994]," Knowlen recalled. "Steve and I had met a year before but we ended up falling in love the first of December. We'd been together a month and a half when I got pregnant in mid-January. I knew because something felt different. Normally I'd get cranky and PMS-y and want to eat Ben and Jerry's ice cream and not do anything nice to my body until starting my period: a day when the world suddenly is a much better place. This felt really different.

"I went into my clinic, actually to get a pap smear. Instead I got a positive pregnancy test. I immediately asked my health-care provider, whom I'd had for a number of years, where I could go to get an abortion."

Knowlen said that "it was a really difficult process this time. I didn't know if I could go through it again. Why? I'm thirty-four. This isn't supposed to happen when you grow up. It's all supposed to be worked out. Because I *am* careful. But the candy store was open on that one occasion and it shouldn't have been, as I told Steve. But you can never count on this stuff. Pregnancy hits you when you least expect it. I'd just lost my job. Steve and I were very much in love, but we were both at a time in our lives when it just wasn't possible to have kids."

Consequently, she said, she didn't even consider maintaining the pregnancy. Her health-care provider gave her a list of abortion clinics.

"I started calling around," Knowlen said. "I remembered hearing about RU-486 in the news. It had been all over the news a few months earlier, but then of course it had gotten very quiet again. I called Planned Parenthood first and they told me that this clinic was testing the drug. So I called.

"I could've scheduled for the following week," she said, "but I decided to wait an extra week. It was before I started getting morning sickness, which is something I don't just get in the morning. I tend to have it all day long. I'm a really unhappy pregnant person. I felt like I really just wanted to sit with it a little longer. It was a part of Steve and me inside of me. I just didn't want to let go of it so easily. I really wanted to take the time to process it.

"I wasn't immediately sold on the pills, either. So I got the names of the drugs. My chiropractor is also a naturopath. So I talked with her about it. She looked up the drugs in the *Physicians' Desk Refer-*

ence, and the second drug—which had been used for bleeding ulcers for ten years—was apparently safe. The information she found about the first one also put me at ease. The drugs also apparently got out of your system very quickly so there wouldn't be any long-term problems about cancer (there's quite a history of cancer in my family) or birth defects.

"So I just wanted to sit with it for a while. It was a really special feeling, even though I knew that I wasn't going to go through with it. It was hard for both Steve and me. He wanted to go to the clinic with me the first day but couldn't. He's a musician and he was playing for a school concert, and there was no way he could get out of it."

Knowlen said she had no way of gauging the advantages of drug-induced rather than surgical abortion until after having experienced both. She recalled no lingering physiological effects from the surgical procedures. Emotional problems?

"No," she said, "because the subject of abortion has always been really, really clear to me. I grew up without a lot of heavy religion in my life. So there wasn't any emotional baggage, like if I had grown up Catholic. I'd never known any of that. I was never even baptized. I think it was really brave of my parents in Connecticut during the 1960s that they chose to give us kids the chance to find our own religion. That was the Connecticut of the blue laws, which said if you weren't married, then you couldn't get condoms. That's why I'm here, by the way.

"But lingering emotional effects? No, I was always just sad getting pregnant because I knew there was no way I could have a child at the time. But I'm also so glad that I have had the choice to make the decision by myself. I mean, pregnant at nineteen? My god. I'd been molested two years earlier, I was at the height of my experimentation with drugs and alcohol and sex and all that crazy stuff you do for a while after high school. So I was lucky to be able to choose abortion, which isn't for everyone. Neither is adoption. For me, there's no way I could give up a kid for adoption. And, even being in love with Steve, I knew this last time that there was just no way

I could have this pregnancy. I feel really strongly about choice. I feel that, if we didn't have this right, then there would be so many other avenues shut down in our lives."

Knowlen noted that what happened with her as a result of Mifepristone treatment was a rarity among women who used the drug at our clinic.

"I passed the entire amniotic sac intact that night," she recalled. "One of the questions they had asked at the clinic was whether I wanted to see the tissue after the abortion. I said I did. I'd done that the first time at Denniston's clinic, and it was really good for me to see that there was this little thing. Anyway, I took the drug at 1:11 P.M., I started bleeding at 4:11. At 8:30 I started bleeding really heavily, passing clots the size of my palm. The one at 8:30 had a lot of tissue, kind of blob-like. I'd asked them at the clinic if they wanted me to save the tissue and bring it in, and they'd said there was no reason to. At 9:30 I passed a clot that was even larger and it was bulbous. I said to Steve: 'Honey, could you bring the container in, this is something.' Steve brought it in. I was sitting in the bathtub, crying. I did a lot of crying that night. When we brought it into the clinic the next day, sure enough, it was the amniotic sac. And we could see the little embryo, which was kidney-bean size. We could see the little yolk sac."

Knowlen and her partner had conducted a "letting-go ceremony" on a beach beforehand. Afterward they returned "to bury everything on the beach. It was about a week afterward. Nobody was around. It was a windy day. We felt the loss.

"Would I use this method again? Yeah, I would. There's a subtle difference that might not be right for other people. This method gave me a lot more time to process what was going on. That was the most important distinction for me. It was a much more active process. When it came down to it—and when you see the video documentary you'll see a reenactment that felt real to me—when it came time to take those pills in that cup, there was no doubt in my mind that I was doing this. I was making this decision, and I was taking these pills that were going to end whatever it was that was going on inside me. And it was really intense.

"With a surgical abortion, it's much more passive. You go into the doctor's office, people are dressed in a certain way, it's very sterile, you lie down, you stick your feet up, and you're vacuumed out. And then you go home. It's over, beginning to end, in thirty minutes. And you can be sedated and totally put under, which would be like having a baby completely sedated: You pass out with a big, huge belly and wake up with this baby in your arms.

"So the active-passive part was a really strong difference for me. Once I took that first pill, of course, that was it, there was no turning back. I was aware of that and I didn't have any qualms. The decision had already been made."

Knowlen had been informed prior to the procedure that it would be free, and granted that "it was a big help. Steve works with kids and he makes like seven bucks an hour. I had just lost my job.

"But I felt and still feel that it is really important to get this drug into the country. Because there are more and more abortion options being shut down. Planned Parenthood has had to replace all the glass in front of buildings with boards because of fear of bombings. I feel this is another good option for women. So far it has shown to be safe, and it's been effective in 99 percent of cases. I felt that if I could help it along by being part of this trial, then that was really important.

"Some friends have told me that my doing interviews is wonderful and brave, and for me it's not that at all. If abortion had not been legal when I first got pregnant, I might be dead now. Abortion in 1980 had only been legal in this country for seven or eight years. I would've been one of those women who, if abortion hadn't been legal, would've sought one out anyway."

Knowlen, who also is an accomplished photographer, recalled recently seeing a photo of a woman who died in the process of an illegal abortion in a New York hotel room.

"She's nude, she's lying down with her legs tucked under her and her face forward. And when I saw her it really hit me: how that could've been me. So I feel that going through these interviews and being public is part of the payback."

Knowlen said she volunteered to be part of the TV project, which included taping women all over the world. She said the producers actually found it easier to locate willing women in India than in the United States. She attributes this reluctance to the present climate of violence against all parties to abortions. And, while her immediate family accepted her decision, she found the reactions of some members "funny," in a sense.

"Mom did really well the first phone call. The second phone call was more focused toward her agenda, as in: 'All my friends are carrying around pictures of their grandchildren. None from you.' I finally talked to her about it, telling her: 'I really didn't need to hear that. I know that's maybe how you feel. But I really didn't need that then.' Then I got a call from my brother in the middle of the night. He lives in the Czech republic. He said: 'Sherry, if the reason you're not doing this is financial, I can help you out.' This is my kid brother, who has a penny, maybe, to his name. I got this E-mail from him that was really sweet about how I'd be a great mom and we can help you out."

What if Knowlen gets pregnant again?

"We're being a lot more careful now," she said. "We were actually using condoms without spermicide, because I'd bought a lot of them. Now we're back to the kind with spermicide. I was on the pill when I was eighteen. It's always done a lot of funny things to me. And I was on it a few years ago for a while. It was just driving me crazy. I felt completely foggy all the time. I had talked with my health-care provider about going on the pill, and she told me that as fertile as I am, I might need to consider it. I talked with Steve and he said, 'Nah, we'll just double up.' When I was on the pill I gained about five pounds, my breasts grew to the size of grapefruits and it wasn't my body anymore. My sex drive went through the roof and there was no one at the time to practice with. It was horrible, I hated pills. It was like being three months pregnant all the time. It just didn't work for me.

"If things were steady between Steve and me, then maybe we'd have a baby. The decision has always been easy in the past. Maybe it won't be so easy next time. But the decision will be mine."

Appendix D

Marsha Jones is a thirty-three-year-old piano instructor. She's single and has no children. At eighteen, while attending college, she became pregnant after admittedly "not using the diaphragm properly. I was just partially educated about how to use it," she said. "You need to reapply the gel and I didn't do it. It just wasn't the right time to have a baby then, so I went to a clinic in Tacoma and got a surgical abortion. It was not too much fun. The experience wasn't what I would call 'horrible,' but it wasn't enjoyable by any means. It was something I never wanted to have happen again. I was fine with the decision. That was the best option for me at the time. But the idea of a needle in the cervix was uncomfortable for me. I had a lot of family support, and I went to a counselor. That obviously helped. But of course I was very young and I wasn't even six weeks along at the time.

"After that I went on the pill, and was on for years and years. About three years ago I finally got off the pill and went back on the diaphragm. Now I'm in a serious relationship, living with my boyfriend. We'll probably get married. But when I got pregnant in early 1995 it still wasn't the right time for either of us to have the baby. We figured if only this had happened in another two years it would be just about right. I just don't think it's responsible to have a baby when you aren't ready emotionally to give what the baby needs. Financially it wasn't right, either. I have a really secure living, but my boyfriend is still going to school. It just wasn't a good time. It would've meant more stress than I felt would be good for a baby."

Jones said it was her doctor at Women's Medical Clinic in Seattle who recommended that she look into having a Mifepristone-induced abortion at our clinic. But Jones had only a vague awareness at the time about such a thing as a drug-induced abortion. She had no idea that it was available at a testing site in the Pacific Northwest.

"I had known about some kind of drug being tested or used in Europe, but didn't know it was here. If I hadn't heard about it, I still would've had a surgical abortion. But when I heard about the drug treatment I was very interested and I called that day. My doctor gave a lot of credibility to the method when she recommended it so highly. And it proved to be a great thing for me: being part of the study, being part of something that was not surgical and the fact that it was free. I didn't know it would be free. My doctor actually said she thought it might be even more expensive than a surgical abortion. If it had been I still would've opted for it, knowing what I know now.

"The information I got over the phone was excellent. They were very, very thorough and helpful. The experience at the clinic was really nice, too, actually: very friendly, thoughtful people. It differed from the 1980 experience in that even the reception room is very warm and comfortable and clean. All the time that was spent with me was very comforting, getting to meet all the women: doctors, nurses. It was just really personable. The first time I went in I was with my boyfriend. I was very nervous, mainly because I had to take a blood test. I'm one of those people who absolutely hates needles and blood tests. I'm terribly squeamish about it. In fact, when I learned that I'd have to have a blood test I thought about not doing the pill if it meant I wouldn't have to give blood. But I told the people there about my squeamishness, and I've never had a more comfortable blood test. Afterward everyone was really kind through the physical and pap smear. They let me look at the little picture (of the conceptus)."

Jones said that during the two days between taking the pills she felt "kind of punky. I wasn't feeling too good, took work off. I just laid around for a few days. At the clinic they had warned me that physically and emotionally it would be like having my period, only about three times worse. So it was kind of emotional and I had cramps. I just kind of felt like curling up on the couch and watching TV. There was discomfort, as though I wasn't quite on top of things.

"Two days later I went in for the second pill. That also wasn't too much fun, but it worked out all right. I had to just hang out at the clinic for about five hours. You could have your friend or boyfriend stay if you wanted, but mine didn't. I sent him away. I just wanted to try to relax, lie down in one of the rooms, maybe get under a blanket and watch TV. And there was more cramping, but it wasn't unbearable. It was just a long day.

"Of course you're supposed to miscarry. But I didn't until I got home that night. When it happened I immediately felt better in a physical sense. Emotionally you just kind of feel: 'Wow, there it is.' It was really amazing to have it naturally induced instead of just having it sucked out of me. My feeling was that, hey, one week of discomfort was worth it as a trade-off as opposed to having a baby. I could sacrifice one week. If I had to do it over again, I'd definitely do it this way as opposed to surgically. It just seemed so much more natural. It was my whole body going through this forced rejection of it, rather than just one area being affected surgically."

She said she felt what she would call "100 percent" physically and emotionally after less than a week. "At the beginning of the next week I felt fine. Now I'm back on birth control. I'd been on the pill for so long, not having to even think about getting pregnant. I guess I was sort of out of touch with my body when I went back on the diaphragm. I thought it was a safe time of the month, but it obviously wasn't. Now I'm just not having intercourse during the time when I'm ovulating."

Jones said on the subject of choice: "I'm absolutely for it. That's one of the reasons I'm so glad that I did it this way. I was hoping I could just help other women in any way, because I'm just so against antiabortion people. They just make me sick. The clinic where I had my first abortion had been picketed, and a friend of mine got quite caught up in the prochoice movement. I ended up writing a letter in support of her cause. My belief now is that more women will opt for using the pill method instead of the surgical. I don't think it's going to just be thought of as an easy birth-control method, because it's not so easy and painless that it could be used that way. And I also think eventually it will cost. Maybe if it were free some women would just consider it to be their method of birth control."

Jones, in any case, already has passed along information about morning-after birth control (discussed in chapter 17) to a couple of friends. One woman was unable to take Jones' advice (possibly, Jones believes, because the friend's pregnancy occurred on a weekend when she couldn't get a prescription for birth-control pills) and later chose to have a Mifepristone abortion. In this way, the word obviously is getting around woman-to-woman about options many of them never knew could exist for them.

Appendix E

Sandy Turner, thirty-four, is a hostess at a Seattle restaurant. She has two daughters, fourteen and nine, and a husband who works in hazardous-waste cleanup. Turner had what she calls a "forced" abortion at the age of fifteen while living with her parents in Alaska.

"It was in Fairbanks. The choice wasn't mine. It was kind of rough. I was too young to know any better, scared, didn't know what to do. So my parents just made the decision for me."

She said the early abortion was traumatic in that her inclination would have been to maintain the pregnancy and give birth. "Even now I wish I had. Nobody likes to give up a baby. But I also knew there was no way that I could have the little one and then give it up for adoption. I just couldn't do that. Ever. I'm a 'Mama' type. But then this second time when I got pregnant, which I never thought would happen again, I knew it would just be too hard on the baby and everybody else. My husband and I had come over here from Montana and we were having to sell things at garage sales as it was just to take care of the two kids we've got. And we both knew we just couldn't start all over again with another baby. Just the expenses of having the baby alone would've been more than we could handle.

"One reason I got pregnant to begin with was that I couldn't afford birth control. What with scraping just to pay for food and clothes for the two kids, there was no way I could pay $25 more a month for pills. Something had to give. I'd been on the pill before and had always had pretty good luck when I went off it. I thought I would be able to tell when the safe times of the month would be. But my husband works odd shifts and it's hard for us to find time to be alone. It just happened."

Turner said she "knew immediately" that she was pregnant.

"When you've been pregnant before, you can just tell. I called up Planned Parenthood. I'd been hearing about the abortion pill for about a year. It's one of those things women sort of keep track of if they think it's going to be something that will help them out. They told me where to call and I called right away. I talked about it with my husband and we both agreed it was the only way to do it. You just get your kids beyond the diaper stage and start to plan for doing things, getting out of the house more. There was just no way at this time for a little one, for starting all over again."

Turner said she was relieved to hear that the Mifepristone treatment would be free. Unfortunately, the treatment didn't work in her case.

"I wanted to try the pill because I figured it might be easier on the body. No type of abortion is easy. Even though they give you painkillers for the suction type abortion, it still can be pretty painful. I remembered my first abortion and what it was like, but if the pill hadn't been available for me I still would've gone ahead with it. So I took the first dose and went home, and everything felt okay. There was a little fluttering in my stomach. I took off work. Then I took off the whole day the second visit, but nothing happened. I went home and rested all weekend and waited, but nothing happened to me. So I called back the clinic first thing Monday and they told me to come in. I had the surgical on Wednesday and immediately felt fine. I went to work the next day."

Turner is adamant about her right to choose an abortion and said she would make the same choice if she were to become pregnant again. She said she is taking extra precautions now to see to it that there isn't another unwanted pregnancy, but also said that her budget hasn't the room for the ongoing expense of birth-control pills.

Her family life also involves another dimension to the subject of sex and birth control.

"I have two daughters, both of them old enough to get pregnant. The fourteen-year-old carries condoms in her purse and probably doesn't like the idea that I know about it. But I'm a lot more open with my girls about sex than my mother was with me. They need to know everything that can happen to them, and they need to know the truth. Otherwise they'll believe whatever their friends tell them—like when they hear that it's impossible to get pregnant your first time having sex. My youngest daughter had her first period when she was only nine years old. She's way too young to know what's going on, but she still needs to know so that she can protect herself. If they don't hear it from someone who knows what they're talking about, then what good is the information? Fortunately my oldest daughter can just go into the counselor's office at school and grab a handful of condoms if she wants.

"It really ticks me off that some people would take away my right and my daughters' rights and other women's rights to make decisions about their own bodies and pregnancies. It's nobody else's business whether you choose to stay pregnant or choose not to. Where does it go from there? Do they start telling you who you can and can't have sex with? Does it get like China, where somebody else decides how many kids you can have?

"I hope it never happens with me again. But if it did, I'd be really glad to know that there was an abortion pill."

Index